Sexuality and Spiritual Growth

Sexuality and Spiritual Growth

JOAN H. TIMMERMAN

CROSSROAD • NEW YORK

1993

The Crossroad Publishing Company
370 Lexington Avenue, New York, NY 10017

Printed in the United States of America
Library of Congress Cataloging-in-Publication Data

Timmerman, Joan H.
    Sexuality and spiritual growth / Joan H. Timmerman.
        p. cm.
    ISBN 0-8245-1137-9
        1. Sex—Religious aspects—Christianity.   2. Spirituality.
    I. Title.
    BT708.T56   1991
    233'.5—dc20   91–26423
                                                    CIP

To Lillian
and
John (in memoriam)

Contents

Introduction 1

1 · *Real Sexuality and Other Concepts* 7

2 · *The Sexuality of Jesus
and the Human Vocation* 26

3 · *Stages in Sexual-Spiritual Growth* 49

4 · *Cycles of Change* 86

5 · *Theology of Spirit* 103

6 · *Being and Doing* 127

Conclusion 145

Notes 147

Index 156

Introduction

She has composed, so long, a self with which to welcome him,
Companion to his self for her, which she imagined
Two in a deep-founded sheltering, friend and dear friend[1]
                                                    Wallace Stevens

Sex is like going to the supermarket: lots of pushing and shoving
and not much to show for it.
                                                    Shirley Valentine

This book has grown from the need, expressed by students and readers of *The Mardi Gras Syndrome* (Crossroad, 1984), for a more extended and experiential development of its premise: that human sexuality can function in human lives as a sacramental reality, that the spiritual significance of our sexual lives and the sexual significance of our spiritual lives need not remain a "forgotten" theological truth. Sexuality is integral to spiritual growth and depends on it. For many reasons, amnesia rather than *anamnesis*[2] has characterized theological thinking about sex. The interconnection, for good or ill, of bodily life with life in the Spirit, once celebrated ritually, was reduced by moralizing to an instrumental connection. Prior to the loss of an idea comes its neglect, the reducing of its value, usually not by an outright falsification, but by stating half a truth as the whole truth. The reductionism characteristic of mid-life disillusionment with sex is aptly expressed by Shirley Valentine's supermarket analogy. Everyone knows the analogy describes a fact of life. But everyone laughs because it is also perceived as only half the truth. What is problematic is that the half truth can be taken as the metaphysical reality for the person who has become disconnected from life, and whose physical expressions have consequently become "empty" symbols, mocking vitality and relationship that is no longer present. Such reductionism is the stuff of humor,

1

of course, and plays a salvational role in human life by showing us objectively, that is, in cartoonlike fashion, what our lives have become. Self-knowledge can precipitate the moment of crisis that helps us reject the caricature in favor of a fuller appreciation of the truth.

But when that reductionism has become uncritically identified with the reality itself; when the reductionism becomes the dogmatically proclaimed and accepted norm by which life itself, not just one stage in it is judged, then, this book will argue, there is no longer salvation (nor humor, nor fact) in it. There is only ideology. The ideology of sex which has been transmitted through church, family, and medical establishments has fractured eroticism from spiritual growth. But that was an ideology constructed to deal with the problems of a certain kind of society, one for whom the threat to its existence was perceived to come from excess of pleasure, from emotional attachments. That interpretation of what endangers human development can and has been deconstructed, to make room once again for a fresh insight into experience. Necessarily a new articulation of the relationship between sexuality and spirituality will have inadequacies, and will need also, eventually and in certain situations, to be ignored, criticized, or debunked. But no one who has ever lived through the unmasking of one ideology, taken uncritically as the truth about human life, will be quite as vulnerable to the absolutizing of another.

All of this is not just clearing the land to make room for a recovered memory, a "new" theory older than the traditional one; it is also a promise and a disclaimer. Theology considers all things in their relation to God. The object of the consideration, "all things," implies that the whole range of human experience is theologically significant, and therefore theological reflection is supremely, even some would say, foolishly confident. But by the addition of the qualifying phrases, "in relation to God," the theological project is also recognized as an enterprise that is consciously self-negating. God as ultimate mystery is not a fact to be mastered or used in instrumental fashion to illumine others. Things in their relationship to God are only known to be such by faith. But faith is a vision without a pointer; it needs words to communicate itself, and words are always inadequate, not just to the divine reality, but even to the finite insight into the Mystery that impels an individual to say what she sees.

Nonetheless, the intent of this book is to suggest a possible form that a theology of the relationship between spirituality and sexuality might take. It is obviously not meant as a "how to" exercise, neither for "spiritual" nor "sexual" athletes. Such manuals abound, but all of them I know proceed from the premise that a person works either at one or the other. Spiritual guides have written manuals of family spirituality, personal spirituality, liturgical spirituality, but not family sexuality, personal sexuality, or liturgical sexuality. Sex therapists and counselors have produced the joy of sex, sex without guilt, and *nouvelle* sex, but none of these proceed on the assumption that there is a connection with Spirit.

For the all-important overturning of assumptions, a theoretical piece is needed: a theology of the relationship between sexuality and spirituality. Without dispensing with intellectual rigor, logical consistency, and the honesty and seriousness without which extended writing is impossible, theoretical reflection, when experimenting with the overturning of even very serious assumptions, can display a certain intellectual playfulness. One *entertains* ideas, to see what happens; one does not force them into service or order them out of the house if they can't fix things. There is a large element of "what if . . ." that can be frightening to people, especially in thinking about sex. Only the reflections, the social constructs about our sexual lives, are at stake in this book. People who fear that "once we start to think about it we will ruin it" apparently do not realize that we live in the ruins of previous thinking about sexuality. Like architectural ruins, it is good to keep our intellectual ruins around to sober and remind us, but we needn't live in them.

The reason for this book is obviously not to discover new facts within a disciplinary specialty. It is rather to suggest an integration of what is known from disparate fields. The process is basically that of turning data into knowledge by placing it in a new context. So it aims to synthesize, to surprise by unconventional juxtaposition, to look for new relationships between parts and the whole, to rethink past and future in relation to the present, and to suggest patterns of meaning that cannot be seen through the lenses of traditional disciplines.

The metaphor that dominates this essay is "Penelope's Robe," a reference to the garment that Penelope, resourceful woman in Homer's *Odyssey*, wove, unraveled, and rewove. The metaphor is not unproblematic, yet it was chosen for its multivalence. The tunic or robe is a Platonic convention for the body and bodiliness; the sexual is often referred to as the "seamy" side of life; the interweaving of the sexual and spiritual is a task seemingly often accomplished but apparently never completed. That which looks like gift at night becomes task again, especially in the clear light of morning. There is, as well, in the image of the garment woven during the day and unraveled each night to thwart social expectations, a kind of parable about the difficulty of connecting the inner and outer, the multiple and the sex-role-stereotyped self. As used here the image is not alleged to be responsible exegesis of Homer's text. Nor should the debate in freshman college classes about Penelope's deficiencies as a literal role model for the modern woman bias the reader against her use in the title of this book. My inspiration comes from the twentieth-century poet, not the ancient author of the *Odyssey*. In many ways the problem of sexuality and spirituality is Penelope's problem: How compose a self, an integral center, before one is pressed into service as mate, mistress, or mother? In Wallace Stevens's poem, "The World as Meditation," Penelope is a composer, creating the world through mental exertion and reflection. Her inner life, imagination, composes both her perceiving self and the other, Ulysses, whose presence she desires. In an act of *anamnesis*, not amnesia, she feels the warmth of the sun ("interminable adventurer"!) on her face at daybreak, and the poet asks: "But was it Ulysses? Or was it only the warmth of the sun on her pillow?" And answers, "It was Ulysses and it was not. Yet they had met/Friend and dear friend and a planet's encouragement/The barbarous strength within her would never fail." So long as the thought keeps "beating in her like her heart," the possibility of connecting of inner and outer, vertical and horizontal, public and private, historical and natural, is present. The heart and the mind do beat together! A colleague who is a classics scholar informs me that Penelope's robe, in the original, was actually woven to be her shroud. Not even this connotation, it seems to me, robs it of its aptness as a symbol of the problem of connecting spirituality and sexuality in the midst of the complicated concreteness of life. Sex and death are interrelated, biologically as well as psychologically. Moreover, both are symbols of union, bringing about the dissolution of boundaries without, I believe, the loss of personal identity. A very great difference between sex and death is the religious construction of death as the ultimate gateway to union with God; sex in Judaeo-Christian culture has not been viewed so happily.

A prefatory word is required about the experiential source for these reflections. While my own experience is not without value, neither is it the source for the explorations in this book. I think as one who lives within the riches and limitations of my own life, but I neither reflect on my own personal experiences, nor take them to be in any way the "raw material" of my thinking about sexuality, nor the model for conclusions that would generalize about the connection between spirituality and sexuality. My experiences are reality checks: they critique and challenge the concepts that have been derived from a richer mix. The conceptual constructs out of which people live are not unidirectional: there is not a direct line from experience to thought (clear, certain) and back to (correct, controlled) experience. If there were, life would be both easier and worse. We could act directly out of our clearest thought (easier) but know that our thinking was no more than the rationalizing of our previous action (worse). Yet there is another reason for insisting on this by now obvious point: My experience is not paradigmatic for you, nor yours for me, nor should we look for another who can show us how to live sexually. This mistake—to assume the conceptual order can and should be instanced literally in the concrete order—has impeded adult moral development and constrained pastoral practice when it has been made.

How, then, does experience, much valued by existentialist, feminist, and liberation theologians alike, figure in this book? Individuals' experiences (through narrative and anecdote) can help disclose the varieties of meaning assigned to human sexual expression. They can also attest to the dividends of happiness and fulfillment or pangs of regret and guilt that have, in individual lives, characterized certain actions and attitudes. As always, these personal documents must be used critically. I will take care not to move from one level of discourse to another, that is, from the conceptual model to the concrete example uncritically. While experience can lead to error, so can every other source of moral understanding, even a direct revelation of God, if it is misinterpreted. The most powerful critique of any ethical use of experience is accomplished by gathering more experience of greater diversity and comparing it with the interpretations already made. Christian thinking about sexuality was always influenced by experience, but most often it has been the experience of attempting to curb and train the sexual impulse within a celibate lifestyle.

The new thing, then, is not the appeal to experience but the two-way process of induction-deduction which is consciously employed. At times certain patterns and their consequences are recognized and illustrated by stories of experience. At other times values, directly disclosed to the individuals in their actions, challenge or reaffirm the traditional namings of value and disvalue. While the examples used are most often from women's experience, it is hoped that they will be of interest and that the theoretical framework employed here will be of use to men as well as women. When we name what we do according to theological categories of grace and sin, both the experiences and the categories are opened to transformation. My hope, in the words of Michel Foucault, is "to change something in the minds of people, . . . to show people that they are much freer than they feel, that people accept as truth, as evidence, some themes which have been built up at a certain moment during history, and that this so-called evidence can be criticized and destroyed."[3]

I am greatly indebted to hundreds of adult students and workshop participants for autobiographical material that they have shared with me and in many cases permitted me to use in this process. Above all, life experience is honored by letting it be what it is: not reducing it by judgment to a category of acts, nor elevating it by arrogance to a norm. To preserve confidentiality, the passages are not directly identified; to acknowledge insight and courage, the authors are here gratefully acknowledged: Rose Mary Boyd, Linda Carey, Cara Lynn Carlson, Robert Cheshire, Irene Eiden, Debbie Eucker, Mary Jo Fortney, Kathleen Hook, Mary Ellen Johnston, Amy Kendall, Theresa Klinge, Doris Knettel, Cheryl Maloney, Judy Nelson, David Osberg, Colleen Riley, Julie Schmidt, Barbara Sheldon, Cynthia Tastad, Beth Tessman, and Kay Trottier.

In addition to the many supportive, encouraging, and challenging students, audiences, and colleagues, I am grateful to my family for ignoring my critics, and to my critics for making it well-nigh impossible for me to stop thinking, talking, and writing about this topic. Finally, it has been a pleasure to be able to count on the superb judgment and consistent challenge that Justus George Lawler offered as mentor and editor in this effort to bring a project of "re-thinking" to some kind of closure. He is without peer in theological publishing, having sought for years to make voices of women audible to hearers beyond the closed circuit of classroom and workshop. Agreement and opposition come cheap as one tries to think the way through a seeming contradiction, but neither manifests the respect for ideas that is represented by this editor's ability to usher them into the arena of public discourse.

1

Real Sexuality
and Other Concepts

Are we perhaps here, just for saying: House, Bridge, Fountain,
Gate, Jug, Olive tree, Window.—possibly: Pillar, Tower? . . .
But for saying them, remember, oh for such saying them, as never
the things themselves hoped so intensely to be. Is not the secret
purpose of this sly earth, in urging a pair of lovers, just to make
everything leap with ecstasy in them?

Rainer Maria Rilke, *Duino Elegies* 9

Both terms, sexuality and spirituality, are ambiguous, not because there is no reality underlying these words, but because there is so much. And because they refer to personal relationships, not to existent objects, they are symbols carrying clusters of meanings. They are not univocal terms, like clitoris or penis, but multivocal or plurivocal terms, like body. This is founded in the complexity of the nature of human action itself, and should not be construed as a reason to avoid speaking about human action named from the points of view of bodily expression or of interpersonal (transcendent) relationship. A reductionist tendency might be identified with both dogmatism and skepticism. Dogmatism: "Why are you trying to make so much of sex; after all, it's just fucking." Skepticism: "Even if you find the spiritual in the sexual, so what? How can I know you didn't just put it there?" Precisely! These are the kind of realities which you won't find there if you don't put them there. Interpersonal reality, the sort of thing called meta-physical by Max Scheler, is not objective. It is intersubjective. We participate in making it what it is for us. Neither sexuality nor spirituality are things out there; they are names for us catching ourselves in the complex act of being human, of transcending the way of being of an object to recognize ourselves as subjects, centers of interdependent activity. I think that both words are resisted with good reason. To mean only coitus when talking about sex is to remain among a field of objects: the woman typically the object of the man; the man typically the object of the desire. To speak of sexuality is not to refer to an "out there," but an "in here," a capacity and faculty, a flexible, formidable way of expressing oneself in one's finitude as male or female. Intercourse, if the term could be reclaimed from the reductionists, suggests the inner, outer and inter-relation of persons. Similarly, to mean only the externals of institutional adherence when speaking of religion is to remain among a field of objects: the faithful as objects of the ministry and teaching; the clergy as instruments of the institution. But real sex includes sexuality, and real religion includes spirituality. Only by falling into reductionism, in the form of objectifying these terms as if they were separate metaphysical entities, have we seen clearly that the return to the point of view of the reflective subject is required.

SEXUALITY

It is essential at the outset to describe what is meant in these pages by bodiliness, so that the hypothesis regarding its connection with spirituality can be understood and tested. I both have and am a body. My body is "both an object for others and a subject for myself."[1] But this ambiguity, that body is capable of two interpretations, is not the same as ambivalence, that there are unresolved conflicts concerning it. Phenomenology has declared the traditional dichotomizing of mind and body as inadequate and inaccurate. So defined that they were seen in a negative relationship—as one was repressed, the other was assumed to thrive—it would be possible to define them so that they were assumed to be identical: your sexuality is your spirituality. But experience does not bear this out, and I do not want to replace a simplistic separation with a simplistic identification. Einstein is reputed to have said that we should try to make things as simple as possible, but not more simple. To affirm a relationship is useless unless it can serve understanding, to work for us to help us resolve conflicts and increase positive experiences. In two ways I hope to do this: first, by attempting not just to define the terms but to describe the human experiences which are their referents; second, to aim not to convince but to explore and to imagine. Proof is not sought, for it cannot be found in an investigation into interpersonal realities. This interpretation is meant to provide a catalyst for self-understanding. It points to examples, discloses values, and hopes to increase the bodily experiences of knowing and loving, of joy, peace, patience, and courage. To that extent these reflections will have been of value. Not the writer, then, but the reader applies the hermeneutical principle.

The dialectic between explanation and understanding, understanding and life traces the "hermeneutical circle" in theology, but according to Paul Ricoeur,[2] while remaining an insuperable structure of knowledge, when it is applied to human things it is not a "vicious circle." It opens out to the illumination of experience; it does not aim to produce a utopia.

In the interest of achieving at least a basic agreement on key terms, I describe as "sexuality" the entire range of feelings and behaviors which human beings have and use as embodied persons in the world, expressing relationship to themselves and others through look, touch, word, and action. It includes the combination of our gender (identity and role) and sex (anatomy and physiology) and is coextensive with personality. Sex, used as an abbreviated term to mean sexuality in this recovered humanistic context, means more than the connecting of organs in genital interaction which acts out natural impulse; it includes the subjective capacity for free and responsive expression of the person, always a bodily, gendered, morally significant response. While sexual vitality is observable in particular organs and their physiological response to stimuli, and is dependent on hormones and physical states, it is not reducible to the material or hormonal level. It is as much an expression of the mind and imagination, knowledge and memory as it is of the glands and muscles, though it is expressed in glands and muscles. Both more and less than genital contact, human sexuality encompasses intention, respect, and intimacy that go beyond and sometimes stop short of the act by which the woman's vagina contains the man's penis. "This is a much broader view than I had previously," wrote one woman. "I think I had very little definition around sexuality outside the sex act. There is a need simply to experience my body in new ways."

Awareness of sex and gender grows with our perception of ourselves and the ways we respond to the messages and expectations of others. When Elizabeth Taylor was quoted as saying, "My beauty is all I ever really had," she was identifying with a pattern, a self-image based on physical features and a sex-goddess stereotype. It is not surprising that, faced with the fact that her "beauty" is gone, she continued her sentence with, "My life is over." Sexuality is certainly mediated by the physical and in turn mediates the spiritual. Sex appeal is the word generally used to register if and how successfully a person's body mediates her sexual potential. Yet mediation is different from equation: physical features have something to do with the whole of life, but one should not be collapsed into the other. The sexual might be said to be in relation to the body somewhat as the mind is to the brain. Yet sexuality is not a function of my body, but larger than my body, a power of my person, as is my intelligence, my will, and my spirituality. Ms. Taylor did not say, "Its life is over," but "my life is over." She was inaccurate in reducing life to physical beauty, but profound in her perception that, once reduced, the reality would shrink to match the perception. There is continuity and coherence, yet not identity between body, sexuality, and spirituality.

As inherent in individual persons, formed and defined within their cultures, human sexuality is not just one's own as subject; it has a history. It does not exist in perfect form in God's mind or will, but its perfection is to be an aspect of changing human persons in a diversity of changing cultures. In classical Greece, for example, some individuals would have been seen as not persons since they did not own (even though they possessed) their bodies. Moreover, they had no legal identity other than that derived from the owner whose property they were. Sexuality, thus, is claimed, as freedom is claimed, not given as are limbs and organs. A dynamic and changing sexuality belongs to culture, not nature. Its dysfunctions can be caused and cured, whether in the personal expression or in the social form, though they are not well understood, because not studied until recently. It is valued and feared and exists under an unwritten rule of silence and secrecy. To break that silence, even in one's own mind, is a fearful thing. This remains true even if Foucault's thesis is accepted, that is, that the past century has produced not liberation but greater control of sex through its constant pressure to confess, analyze, and subject bodily activity to scientific study. I would agree that once sexual feeling has been translated into discourse, it can be used to extract the information needed to control. But I do not see the return to secrecy or ignorance as a desirable way to avoid that dilemma. Expressiveness is also an effect (and purpose) of human discourse. If someone is unable to conceptualize aspects of himself apparent to others, he is more, not less, vulnerable to control by others who are more knowledgeable. Students routinely tell of the conflicts they undergo merely telling their parents and friends that they are taking a college course with the word *sexuality* in the title.

> I have learned throughout lecture and group discussions that sexuality can be discussed in a fun way. That we can laugh at silly puns; that sex, when discussed, does not have to be solemn and boring. Sex talk can be interesting, enlightening, and fun. That was really refreshing for me. I am so used to people being so uncomfortable when discussing it.

The fear appears to be that of acknowledging themselves as sexual subjects, legitimate heirs to a history of human wisdom regarding the confused desire they feel.

Heretofore the "history" of human sexuality, formally as an account of human becoming or informally as stories of personal pain and fulfillment, remains unwritten.[3] So long as this is the case, individuals feel isolated and alone, each imagining herself odd and inadequate for a different set of reasons, while the idealized sexual existence remains unattainable.

> "I stayed in that marriage in a victim role," one woman wrote. Always being duped into thinking things would get better. His goal was to keep me satisfied sexually. That was our only means of communication. He did an outstanding performance on that score. Sex was the only real focus. Touch led to orgasm and magnificent mutual satisfaction, all in one breath, it seemed. And then I was left empty. There was talk, but no communication. There were decisions, but no mutuality, discussion or sense of equality. The sexual focus sucked the spirit out of me.

If the ideal attempts to overcome all desire with rationality, the ideal is unattainable; if it identifies satisfaction with being insatiable and multi-orgasmic, it is also unattainable. Either way the false ideal functions effectively as a source of guilt and victimization rather than as the common human symbol of connectedness and mature vitality.

Sex is good. At first sight the linking of these three words might appear to be the ultimate in naiveté or the useless restatement of the obvious, yet these three words need to be linked together in a theological context to counter an ancient amnesia. "And God saw that it was good . . ." is the recurring motif of the creation story.[4] God declared "good" the light, the earth and sea, the plants, fruits and seeds, and "every living creature that moves." God "blessed" them with reproductive capacity and said "let them multiply on the earth" (Gen. 1:21–22). God then created human being, male and female he created them, and blessed them as well so that they might "fill the earth and subdue it" (1:28). "And God saw everything . . . and, behold, it was very good" (1:31). From this version of the creation story there is no doubt and no ambivalence: the sexual potency of all earth creatures is in continuity with the creativity of the divine source of all being. It is "very good." But now, calling attention to that tradition in the context of later theological development, one appears to have to protest too much, to be open to challenges of naiveté. The burden of proof has been shifted by the version of the next story in Genesis—a story widely characterized as that of the "Fall" and dominant in the Judaeo-Christian de-valorization of sexuality. The second story has so associated male and female sexual awareness with the connotations of danger and sin that the other half of the truth, sexuality as mediation of life and love, has been deprived of a hearing. "Sex is good," says the Creator in the first story; "Objection" says the interpreter for the second; "Sustained," says the theological judgment of the authoritative church of the recent past. The difference between the first and second story is not in being but in "knowing." Reflective sexuality is the blessing and curse of the second version: "And the Lord made for Adam and for his wife garments of skins, and clothed them, Then the Lord God said 'Behold, the man has become like one of us, knowing good and evil. . .'—therefore the Lord God sent him forth from the garden of Eden, to till the ground from which he was taken" (3:21–24). The fruit of the tree of knowledge is ambivalence: one knows oneself as not only made but clothed by God. Now the gift has become task. Once outside the garden of direct vision, the woman and the man might remember that there is a tree of Life, but the religious voices they have internalized have declared an enmity between the holy and the human, between the sacred and the sexual, between the playful and the prayerful.

As many commentators have observed, the negative sexual attitudes associated with the Christian tradition are not required by the Genesis text; they evolved during the first four centuries of theologizing. They drew from—and departed from—pagan practices, Jewish tradition, and memories of Jesus. The desire for heroic virtue was expressed by Christians in their embracing of celibacy even as their predecessors had embraced martyrdom. They considered themselves the timeless "people of the resurrection" (Luke 20:36) who were not bound by the social structures represented by marriage. The tension between the heroic, prophetic forms of Christian living and the common, sacramental form has not yet been resolved, especially and most painfully with regard to the inescapable dependencies of food and sex. Was such dependency to be feared and fled or to be embraced and transformed? To be free of need and desire was the human ideal articulated by Jewish Essenes and Stoic philosophers. Since appetite grows even as it is fed, sex and food stood as a symbol of humiliation to those who defined being human as being beyond physical desire.

Elaine Pagels has shown convincingly that what was at stake in the early Christian articulation of its new anthropology was freedom. While some radicals among the early Christian thinkers interpreted the reason for the banishment of Adam and Eve as illicit sexual activity, the majority of commentators on the Scriptures viewed it as an act of disobedience, thus implying that human beings were created responsible for the choices they are able to make freely. Had Adam and Eve been merely rebuked like children, she argues, the impression would have been that they were unable to control the forces that took over in them. Human responsibility, not human corruptedness, is affirmed by the serious consequences described in the story. The assumption that freedom, rather than the disability consequent upon the Fall, was the point of the theology of creation is reflected also in Clement of Alexandria's claim that the equality of all persons created in God's image constituted a religious reason for rejecting the civic obligation to worship the emperor. For him and others, the Genesis story was not primarily the story of an irreversible loss of trust, but a parable of responsibility. It has been interpreted since in such a way as to become the basis of western ideas of the dignity and equality of human persons, and eventually to be given political currency in the ideal of democratic self-government. Over against the gnostic Christians who denied that baptism fully delivered the faithful from sin and suffering, there were those who referred to themselves as orthodox and reaffirmed the completeness of the victory of the redemption over the Fall. Most convincing to me is that they argued to the thoroughness of redemption from the teaching on the efficacy of baptism. But how did they get from the idea that baptism constituted them as a community of free persons, not slaves to anything, to the notion that normal sexual activity should be foregone? It is easy to understand how the leap of faith would lead the most ardent of the new converts to accept that "renouncing the world" of Roman privilege was the way to realize the greatest freedom. The form that renunciation took, historically, was in the rejection of householder status—with its inevitable concern for the accumulation of material goods. The decision to establish a family requires the means to support it. Because the means of conception control were not known, freedom to make other decisions became moot once the decision to be sexually active was taken. Only in the last forty years has that situation changed for a substantial part of the population.

Asceticism became the means to the Christian goal of the freedom of the new people of God. The ascetics interpreted Genesis according to their own lights, yet they did not diverge from the common tradition of the first four hundred years of Christian thought: that freedom in its many forms, including self-mastery as the source of freedom, was the primary message of the story of creation, ritualized in the waters of baptism. Why then is the burden of proof now on those who would assert the compatibility of sexuality with goodness? Why has sexuality become implicated as both cause and effect of sin and death?

The religious valorization of sexuality, as well as the inherited meaning of baptism, changed through a process that is usually attributed to Augustine. Instead of a story of the misuse of moral freedom which explained the physical death of Adam's descendants, Augustine was instrumental in re-imagining it as an account of the irreversible corruption of man's experience of sexuality. Rather than the misuse of his capacity for moral freedom, its loss was chronicled. Paul's letters did not identify sexual disorder as a consequence of the Fall, nor was it a common interpretation of Genesis by the Christian thinkers and teachers of the first four centuries. Nowhere in the Hebrew Scriptures is there to be found speculation on a causal connection between concupiscence and original sin. The more common reflection on concupiscence is that of Philo, which traces it to unreasonable desires which can be brought under control by asceticism aided by human contemplation of divine law. Augustine's theory of original sin, with its presumed effect of weakening the human will and unleashing the passions, was articulated as the inspired message of Genesis and Paul's letter to the Romans (5:12—"Therefore as sin came into the world through one man and death through sin, and so death spread to all men because all men sinned"). As a theological construct the importance of alleging sexual transmission as the manner in which sin and death spread to all can hardly be overstated. Contemporary translations from the original, to which Augustine admittedly had no access, make it clear that death spread to all because all "sinned," not because all were propagated by sexual interaction. Moreover, there is not even the slightest hint in Romans of sin expressing itself more readily through sexual interaction. Nor is ascetical renunciation of sexual pleasure viewed as the means of redemption (Rom. 5:19—For as by one man's disobedience many were made sinners, so by one man's obedience many will be made righteous). It is amazing that such a construct based on inaccurate exegesis so authoritatively took over the field, but even more so that it blocked from memory an older Christian anthropology based on co-creativity with God and responsibility for relationships with other creatures. The effect, certainly not attributable to one thinker, was a view of human nature that served the political purposes of those who governed, both state and church. If human beings, as victims of concupiscence, are universally in need of external controls, then they, and surely their sexuality, must be managed by others.

When people object to the statement that sex is good, their resistance comes elsewhere than from primary experience. Daily life tells us that everything has its moments of light and shadow, its built-in rewards and penalties for use and abuse. The context in which sexual fulfillment or frustration is first observed affects how we feel about it. When longing for love appears to produce only tears and pain in an older brother or sister, sex might well appear overvalued to the younger sibling. By contrast when vitality and excitement accompany the sexual messages in music or in the life expressions of those around us, the effect is positive. The exegesis of daily life carried out by even the least thoughtful would suggest that sexuality is in itself neither the problem nor the solution. There is rather a pervasive ideology about the danger of sex, supported by selective theological and biblical interpretation, that has oversimplified sin and elevated control of sexual desire to high virtue. But the desire for control is itself a form sin takes. There are hermeneutical choices to be made. Interpretation is not arbitrary, but neither is the traditional alignment of sin with sex required by an order of facts or logic. Historical research has taken the ground from under the religious anthropology that would identify sexual pleasure with the Fall. If neither experience nor doctrinal consistency requires it, how can the persistence of a negative view be accounted for? I think the most adequate explanation is to understand the constraints against sex as a pedagogical fiat that was useful for particular social and political benefits but outlived the system for which it was a creative adaptation. It lingers as a "what" whose "why" has been forgotten. In fact, in the emerging context, one characterized by equality between men and women, reliable means of conception control, and an educated general population, such negating attitudes serves exactly opposite ends. Rather than cooling the disorderly impulse, the prohibitive mentality stimulates it through false guilt and the lure of the forbidden. Moreover, it keeps the emphasis on externals and actively prevents the transition to internal self-discipline. Thus sexuality is excluded from the Christian sacramental experience of newness and freedom, and ignored as a paradigm of life in the Spirit. More will be developed on this alternative in chapter 5, in which spiritual growth and moral decision-making is explored.

Even after explanations such as the above, it is disturbing to many to hear the words *sexuality* and *spirituality* put in immediate proximity to each other. When a course in theology bearing the title "Spirituality and Sexuality" was proposed, the spontaneous expressions of discomfort ranged from "Why" to "How?" to "Here?" The first papers, reflections on five things still believed and five no longer believed from early teaching about sex, included statements such as these:

> My sexual self has been misused, abused and then abandoned in a void of anorexia. Once I knew only the destructive potential of human sexuality. Now I embrace it as an integral part of my desire and capacity to love.
>
> My sexuality was not just created for childbearing but also for my good feelings about myself. This does not always require another person to be with me, it's something I don't have to save until someone comes along to "start." It's mine.
>
> How can we study sexuality and spirituality? I thought at the beginning. Now I realize one is not a fully completed part of me without the other.

There are, of course, good reasons for the initial skepticism raised by my hypothesis explored in the following chapters: that spiritual growth and sexuality are not only connected but causally connected, and that one's understanding of the way they are related to each other determines one's experience. Among those reasons the following should at least be listed: failure to do enough "soul searching" in the midst of living; fear of extremism, absence of positive models for either spiritual growth or sexual fulfillment; psychological images of an integrated personality that exclude the bodily; disillusionment with ideals that sound like challenges to self-improvement, and a sense of alienation, of powerlessness, with regard to both. I get up in the morning, but my "sexuality" does not. It may or may not overtake me sometime during the day. I do a good day's work but my "spirituality" does not accompany me; at best it bids me good-bye and greets me again at the end of the day. The message of this book is that I am my sexuality and my spirituality. Far from being two incompatible powers warring over me, I, performing myself, am—in relation to human persons and to the divine calling from within and without. I am not dual, body in opposition to spirit; nor am I simple; I am multifaceted, living out multiple aspects of life in the only way possible to finite being, one at a time. Running has often been used as an image of the spiritual journey. In the following, a student reflects on running as the catalyst for raising to awareness the sexual character of nongenital experience.

> Is this a sexual experience? No doubt about it! I feel my breasts, my hair, and all the muscles in my body bouncing with the move-ment. . . . I feel the sweat trickling down my stomach and behind my ears. I see other runners going by and I know the pleasure they feel in the movement. . . . And then I pass a walker and I feel eyes on me from behind. It's exhilarating; it's energizing; it's sensual; it's sexual; it's creative; it's spiritual. . . . When I'm running, I'm free, I'm entire. When I'm running, I'm praying.

SPIRITUALITY

Why, if resistance to the possibility of integrating sexuality into a con-scious spiritual life is so persistent, does this book insist on connecting them, at least conceptually? Because good theology requires it. Just as sexuality has forgotten its transcendence, so has spirituality, read narrowly, historically, as monasticized spirituality, lost sight of its immanence. Geoffrey Wainwright, borrowing from Richard Niebuhr's typology of the relations between Christ and culture, identified five types of "the combination of praying and living which is spirituality." In the first type, *Christ-against-Culture,* the world and the flesh are seen as hostile to the cause of God. This type of spirituality is world-renouncing and hostile to the flesh. God's love is thought to be discontinuous with human love. It proclaims respect for the distance between the divine and the human, a distance which, even by grace, is never bridged. Tertullian evidences the Montanist (rigorist) form of this spirituality, and some of the early desert-dwelling hermits exemplify its counter cultural quality. Separatist movements, whether feminist or pentecostal, might provide more current examples of this paradigm.

The second type represents a pendulum-swing to the other extreme: simplistic affirmation of the world. The *Christ-as-Culture* model collapses the spiritual into the cultural. It affirms simple identity rather than differentiated continuity. In this model there is no need for faith and no hope for transformation. Early examples might be the Christianity of the Constantinian empire, in which to be a good citizen was to be a good Christian and vice versa, or the fundamentalist theocracies of the contemporary Middle East. This form has, interestingly enough, a lawless as well as an "establishment" form. Some apologies for celibacy as well as some love-cults could exemplify the type's tendency to identify the text with the context.

The third model is that of *Christ-above-Culture*. It emphasizes the positive elements in human nature, while recognizing that even these need to be purified. "Grace comes to perfect nature," articulates the relationship that is envisioned. This is the model of spirituality of Clement of Alexandria and Thomas Aquinas, where Christ is seen as transfiguring nature forever. Contemporary examples would include some support group programs which rely on a "power greater than oneself" to save the person from her worst possibilities. Most forms of New Age spirituality would exemplify the tendency of this model to identify the sources of power as outside the individual (the crystal, the forces of nature, psychic powers as personalized).

Fourth, some spiritualities acknowledge *Christ-and-Culture-in-Paradox.* This model is dualist in pitting the world against holiness, but is not so extreme as the first model. It sees the dialectic between the earthly and the heavenly. Augustinian and Lutheran spirituality serve as examples, where the polarities are between law and gospel, justice and mercy, and the two kingdoms. The spirituality is consequently characterized by conflict and images of struggle and warfare. This model would certainly attract the "twice-born" personality, identified by William James. It is a most attractive model, especially to the contemporary person who has unmet needs for adventure, danger, and heroic aspirations. Some forms of charismatic and community based spirituality represent this model in the contemporary world.

The fifth and final model is designated *Christ-the-Transformer-of-Culture.* It is founded on a positive doctrine of creation and incarnation, yet affirms the reality of redemption. Conversion and rebirth are needed, but not to replace the natural with the supernatural or to negate the material by spiritualizing it. John Wesley is offered as a theological example. Liturgically the Catholic sacramental system presents a practical implementation of this form of spirituality, in which the reality of grace in history is celebrated. There is more continuity than discontinuity, as the nearness of the divine is affirmed. Still, grace originates not from human or historical sources, but from the divine Spirit. Each model would find a particular name for God, such as Judge,

Father, Savior, Love, more compatible than others. Each would also develop, quite consistently, a particular way of articulating the relationship or lack of it between sexuality and spirituality. The Christ-against-Culture model would find them mutually exclusive; Christ-within-Culture would identify them uncritically (positively celibacy is holiness, negatively sex is sin); Christ-above-Culture would insist on the superiority of the spiritual though it would allow a purified sexual life as compatible with it. Christ-and-Culture-in-Paradox would emphasize the struggle and conflict, worrying and admonishing restraint even while accepting the inevitability of their interaction.

I am convinced that a healthy spirituality adequate to a healthy sexual life can be best conceived broadly according to the fifth model. In one word, it is a sacramental spirituality. It is a superior conceptual model because it sees all love as continuous with God's love and sexual life as transformative of all life. It includes openness to reality in *all its dimensions,* and accepts as foundational the understanding that all things are interconnected. This would require a radical departure from the present compartmentalized ways of looking at things. The mind-body dichotomy, the separation of the spiritual from the secular, of instrumental knowledge from expressive, of masculinity from femininity has resulted in a world that is lonely, violent, and never at peace because always in conflict with aspects of itself. Spirituality does not deal with the top half of reality; it deals with the whole of reality as it is, without artificially imposed compartments. The description brings to mind Frank Sheed's equation of faith with sanity, for sanity is *seeing what is there,* and the divine is there.

Conceptualizing sexuality in its fullest reality should include spirituality, and vice versa. It is simply a fact of experience, though usually noted only after breakdown or illness, that nobody lives well who is not spiritually well. For human beings to stay fully alive, they need to feel a connection with the cosmic, the sacred, the mysterious, the transcendent. To deny the spiritual while developing the sexual, or to cultivate the spiritual at the expense of one's own or another's sexual well-being is to continue the questionable view that the spiritual and sexual operate in separate realms. The concern for authentic spirituality does not mean false innocence, fear of desire or pleasure, or the avoidance of the moral risk characteristic of adult life. What it makes possible is a new perspective on desire and pleasure, a new openness to experience, and an effort to *be* as well as *have* one's body as sacrament and means of worship.

One could characterize the spiritual life as the conversation, sometimes interrupted, sometimes lively, but always ongoing with that Unknown with which the known is connected. It is what we reach for when, in music or art or love or sport or work, we aim for more. Spirituality is the response of the whole person, body, mind, feelings, relationships, to the perceived presence of the holy in the here and now. This response need not be formulated in theological terms, in fact it need not be explicitly theistic in the sense of faith in a personal God. I want, in this book, however, to affirm that connection in the most explicit fashion I can, in continuity with a community and a tradition. So my language is in the language of Catholic theology. Even within that ancient language, spirituality is a new tongue, and is finding only haltingly, an appropriate vocabulary, inclusive and reflective of diversity of lifestyles. Theological language can infuse wonder into the process, as well as a sense of being part of a great procession of seekers for God, by naming the response and its source. The whole person can only be marshalled by something greater than herself that is not separate from herself, that is, by the immanence of God, the Holy Spirit of God, in her sanctifying presence.[5] God, whatever the Ultimate Reality is called in a particular tradition, is the source and goal of all spirituality. That one has been personally addressed by "the center which is everywhere" is made intelligible by faith. But faith does not dictate the response: while evoked by the powerful inner experience of having been called by name, the content of the response is utterly free and spontaneous. Stories of individual persons show the diversity of the response—from the social activism of Dorothy Day to the cultivation of detachment of Etty Hillesum to the eccentric brilliance of Simone Weil. But only the extraordinary stories are generally available. What the common person needs is to compare notes with colleagues in the Spirit.

Spiritual traditions identify not only types of spirituality but stages of growth into the transformed life that has characterized those who knew themselves to be in some way grasped by the Spirit. There have been many different images—ladder, journey, spiral, mountain—by which the insight has been expressed that the spiritual life is dynamic. To speak of its progress in stages only claims analogy with the recent and well-received characterizations of how psychological and moral development is achieved. In this formulation I will list as stages the recognizable moments of the spiritual growth process, combining the insights of various writers in such a way that seems to me to give a relatively complete and contemporary rendering. My intention is to suggest that the spiritual life is composed, that is, it could be imaged as an interwoven fabric in which a strand, once begun, is never completely left behind, but becomes part of the larger "robe" one weaves.

In the first stage, the person has learned to live in a world of things, effectively linking means to ends, managing nutrition, technology, personal energy. This is not to be despised, for without it, all hope of further enhancement of life is unlikely. The first step on a stairway is foundational for it sustains all the rest. It is not dispensable. "Be normal" is the first rule of the spiritual life, according to Jesuit scholar and expert on the Christian spirituality of the East, Thomas Spidlik. It is this stage, and the real joy of learning to manage in a world of things as a responsible adult, that was analyzed as missing in most middle-class American women's lives when *The Feminine Mystique* came upon the scene to inaugurate the women's movement. Not having a job or a career that is valued by society is a spiritual deprivation when it means the individual remains financially and socially dependent and morally infantile.[6]

Stage two is characterized by conversion to a world of people. The second rule of the spiritual life is "Reach out to others." In this stage a real shift of values takes place in which human happiness, relationships, and vitality are assigned priority over the demands of the nonpersonal sphere. This conversion is necessary even if the things valued previously were spiritual riches rather than material possessions. Many films and novels focus on this particular shift, where typically an I-Thou experience, sometimes an experience of romantic love, always an experience of intimacy, breaks into one's life, dividing what is truly meaningful from what is not. For some individuals, this stage is fully negotiated only when they become parents and find the absolute value of human life symbolized in the bodies and lives of their own children. This acknowledgement for another creature of unconditional significance is a sign of true spiritual growth and is not to be scorned. "In itself this step is small," writes Solovyov, "but without it nothing more advanced or greater is possible."[7] At this second stage of spiritual growth the disciplines required for communication, the skills necessary for self-revelation (not just informational language) and listening are developed. The habits required for living in a world of people provide the structure of asceticism in this strand. It is possibly the stage in which most people, especially most conventionally religious people, live the whole of their lives. It is not often said that social etiquette and common courtesy are of spiritual significance, but they are. Moreover, the virtues appropriate to each stage continue through those that follow. This comment is made simply to correct any impression that one "graduates from" or exits the previous stage when one is impelled into the next. Courtesy is included in charity, not superceded by it; self-love is still present as a strand of the cloth of neighbor-love.

In stage three a process of purification is embraced. Old patterns of thought and action that have become obstacles to the call heard in the heart are let go. Social sins, accepted with ordinary socialization, such as misogynism, racism, workaholism, low self-worth, laziness, and half-heartedness are recognized and overcome. The call to take hold of life—to learn to live with enthusiasm using all the senses, to learn to be responsible as a member of the world community—is heard and followed. In this stage a mentor is most important and often appears as if in response to one's desire for direction and growth. The issue is discernment. If the person whose need is to "let go" has bad advice and continues to act on an assumption that spiritual growth is taking on more and more, he is likely to be a candidate for burn-out rather than holiness. For the one who has always seen the spiritual life as the giving up of things, the call to engage in a passionate way may go unheard. At this point in spiritual growth, the balance is sought, the overdevelopment is curbed, the underdeveloped aspects of one's physical and psychological self are accommodated.

Stage four has traditionally been named enlightenment or illumination for it is characteristically a time of vision and revisioning. It may very well coincide with what has been called the age of grief, the time, most often during mid-life, but occasionally earlier in a particularly tragic or traumatic life, when the emptiness of one's present life is revealed. That may be a life whose activities are superficial: the pursuit of privacy and the making of money, but it may also be the inner disclosure of what is still lacking in a life which looks very full of spiritual and physical achievements. The vision may restore the depths of fear and mystery and death, banished by distractions and multiple good works, or it may open one to see the connectedness of things and to awaken an explicit desire for a relationship with the divine. One thing is certainly true, if one turns from the entrance to the illuminative way back to the certainties of a narrower, shallower existence, the rest of life may be safer and more familiar. If I know what is being asked of me, I will do it, says the desire to grow of stage three. The spiritual challenge of stage four is that what is asked of me is precisely to move into the unknown. Leaders like Martin Luther King and Dorothy Day can be recognized at the threshold of this stage. While in retrospect it produced the luminosity that guided them for the rest of their lives, it was experienced in the present as darkness. A frequent metaphor for the way it feels at the time is the metaphor of "hitting the wall," or not being able to see a way over or around, of not being able to continue to act on the strength of usual decision-making processes and sources of energy. Only with the surrender of all self-sufficiency is the light restored and the wall shown to be an opening to a new way of being and serving.

Stage five culminates in union; that is, the person lives as one transformed, in authentic connectedness with the Whole, with an awareness of the Mystery in all things. Authentic, as used here, does not imply flight into the natural from the supernatural. It implies wholehearted dedication and submission to the specifically human, the specifically finite task of a given person's life. Death itself is regarded no longer as the enemy, but as a moment in which the process of transformation, both here and beyond, is continued. Mystical or semimystical experiences are characteristic of union. These, in some lives, have been extraordinary and dramatic; but there is also a mysticism of everyday things. Specific to mysticism is that it carries its own absolute validation; one knows that one has gone beyond, even in the midst of everyday things, what can be described with everyday words.

By considering the emergence of the spiritual life among us as a common and expected dynamic, not solely the experience of the elite, I in no way mean to say that one slides easily into it or from stage to stage within it. All aspects of evolution, as of growth, require leaps, decisive breaks, conversions. The means by which some express these turning points may be less dramatic and discontinuous with their normal cultural pattern than others, but metanoia is common to all. There is a no-saying that comes at every crucial point; it reflects an experience of conflict within the self, sensing two possibilities: the yes to the future is conditional upon the no to the past. But even psychology tells us that conflict is not the enemy; from it character is unified in a new way. The mature man or woman of the Spirit arises out of the antagonism between what is given and what has not yet been imagined.

Both spirituality and sexuality have to do with power. A person with an unexamined mind is powerless in the face of emotional upheaval, role stereotyping, the failure of relationships and the absolutized demands of love. She has not developed the quiet detachment necessary to make personal choices. Not in possession of her soul, she certainly does not possess her body. One's inner and outer power are inescapably linked. To bring about change—in self-esteem, in attitudes toward relationships, in world view—requires attention to moments of spiritual danger and opportunity. Spiritual growth may be no more than making the effort to activate the processes which will lead to that change. Spirituality, as a transreligious concept and a way of life, has been central to the women's movement, not least of all by awakening many to their fundamental oneness with nature, and urging openness to new sources of power.

Sexual life is one such source of power. The first necessity in a process that would lead to integration is an emotional act—to understand and accept bodiliness and sexuality. The second is a spiritual act—to imagine a potential new way of being sexual and whole. The third is to experiment ritually and literally with combining them both. No doubt such a development, necessarily social as well as personal, will be dependent on individuals' willingness to be unconventional, to free their imaginations and memories for new ways of being "people of the resurrection." Since our religious and cultural memory is so devoid of models of bodily spirituality, we may have to invent them.

SACRAMENTALITY

Basic to all religious insight, certainly not just Catholic sacramental theology, is the recognition of the spiritual dimension in all human experience.

In this sense the sacramental principle is the most ecumenical idea around. Denominational refinements and disagreements arise in the attempt to articulate and establish as doctrinal what this "spiritual dimension" is (that is, what it resembles in the interpersonal order, since all theology is analogical and all doctrine was once theology). Moreover, we differ, eventually disagree, and sometimes decide to part ways on the practical issues: how it should be proclaimed and celebrated, and how it can better our lives.

Generally speaking, when the term "sacrament" is used, the reference is to the ritual acts of the institutional churches, whether the definition is that of the Council of Trent, as outward sign, instituted by Christ, to give grace, or that more common after Vatican II: the official action of the people of God which mediates an encounter with God in Christ. In either formulation the focus is on the ceremony or the "religious" action. By sacramentality I describe rather the truth which is the condition for the possibility of the effectiveness of the ceremony; that is, the Mystery of God is present and accessible through the Spirit who, as the Immanence of God, permeates all things. The coinherence of God in matter and history precedes all communication about this presence and human modes of perceiving it. This broader way of understanding sacramentality is also the earlier one. The Western church narrowed the understanding of sacrament to the church and its functions after the twelfth century separation from Eastern traditions in which "sacrament" can apply appropriately to any manifestation of God in human life.

Vatican II in *Gaudium et Spes* broadened the scholastic concept of sacrament by referring to the church as Sacrament. This was particularly significant in the light of the fact that for this document the preferred content of the term "church" was people of God, a return to the early Christian insight that the Mystical Body was the Ecclesial Body. That does not mean to say that there is an eighth sacrament, in addition to the official seven. It means that in this broader sense the term sacrament should not be used in the plural at all. The many rituals are performances of the one sacrament in specific contexts of human need. By using the term sacrament in this theological sense, we recover it in its original use in patristic theology, where *sacramentum* is the Latin word used to translate the Greek *mysterion*. The early structure of the church is sacramental, the Western church would say; in the language of the Eastern church, it is "mystical," that is, it carries the Mystery of God's presence and action into the temporal dimension.[8] This does not mean that it is something abstruse or impossible to understand; it means rather that a hidden-from-the-senses transcendent divine reality reveals itself in a visible way. It is the people who are "mystical." The natural action or element is capable of such disclosure of the divine to the extent that it is "open," that is, to the extent that it is ecstatic, free, not closed in upon itself.

Christian understanding of spiritual formation is incarnational. That means that freedom, ecstasy, openness are performed in the flesh, not by escaping from it. By God's entry into human being, all being, history and nature, is potentially transformed. All reality becomes mediator of Mystery, thus sacramental, to those who can see. All nature is graced. It is important to be explicit here: though the sacrament mediates a 'divine reality through a human potential, this nonetheless remains human. My humanity includes not just what I am at the present moment, but what I can be. I am also my future. To exclude the potential from the real, and identify the real only with what is already actualized is another form of reductionism. The sacramental view of reality is an inclusive view; it includes the Mystery of God as manifested in "natural," that is, sensuously experienced reality. Moreover, a sacramental view recognizes the presence of God mediated not only through the Body (of the Church), but through the body (of the human being); that is, it is communal without thereby relinquishing its personal, intimate, physical locus. The "dialectic of the sacred" is what makes sacramentality different from magic. Because the sacred is revealed through the natural without ceasing to be natural, it can be explained without reducing it to a merely psychological event. It would be nothing more than a psychological event if we understood ourselves to be acting "as if" God's presence were mediated through sexual experience, thus bringing about a new mental attitude. Nor have we need of an explanation that self-destructs into the claim that this is a miracle. By accounting in this way for the revelation of the sacred through natural things, God so takes over the penultimate reality that it ceases to function as itself, and is set aside for purely divine use. Both of these are nonsacramental approaches to material reality. Either God is not really there or the natural reality of bread or body can't still be there. The pendulum in the history of religious practice regarding baptism and the eucharist has swung back and forth between psychologism and a magic miracle mentality—between rituals of mere fellowship and automatic dispensing of grace. Either-or approaches are far more believable to the moralist, rationalist, and supernaturalist mentality of contemporary religious practice than the both-and commitments of the sacramental view.

The scandal of the incarnation and the eucharist is also the "scandal" of sexuality as a path for spiritual growth. For such ideas to take hold, the dualistic mentality has to be let go. Actually, a proper theological understanding of sacramentality relates the polarities, without suppressing the tension between them. It affirms that God's presence is not invented by mental gymnastics but is really real: Christ's divinity in humanity is its warrant. Through the Spirit the Incarnation is extended and is in reality present among us. That presence does not communicate itself automatically because like all personal interaction, it has no objective existence; it has intersubjective existence. Like a kiss it does not exist objectively, waiting in a room to be automatically dispensed when people enter. It is a form of self-gift, of presence, depending for its efficacy not just on the action of the giver but also on the receiver. It is, in Rilke's words, a "transformation of the visible world outside us into an invisible world within."[9] So it would be false, because affirming more than the truth can bear, to say that God is "present" in sexual life. If the sacramental understanding is absent or misrepresented, God's gracious self-giving will not be found to be present. The last thing that this book intends to do is promote a new brand of intellectual gymnastics or moralism by which people would learn to pretend what is not experienced. An honest response to a more complete view of reality is what is urged.

A sacramental view of sexuality requires the reflective inclusion of the spiritual dimension already there; a sacramental theology requires the inclusion of sexuality. The sacramental potential of sexuality does not mean that it is to be taken out of this world into some kind of specially "religious" cult. Karl Rahner perceived the sacramental event, not as a movement from church to world "saving it," but a movement of the spirit leading from the world, that is, from the innermost personal center of those who are its thinking subjects, carrying normal human secular life to its fulfillment in God. Put more practically in regard to sexuality, this means that the dynamism of sexuality itself reveals the holiness of human beings and the world in its very secularity.

A Peanuts cartoon strip (by Charles Schultz) shows Linus at the piano. As he plays, the notes of music flow; Snoopy, lying on the doghouse, perceives not notes but dogbones. That is sacramentality. God's self-expression is rendered in our dimension in a mode that we can appreciate . . . as the desire of our hearts, whatever form it may take.

FOCAL POINTS:

Sexuality is a name given to the whole human person considered from the perspective of embodiment; spirituality is a name given to the whole human person considered from the perspective of orientation toward transcendent meaning.

The history of human sexuality portrays a range of action, some considered normative, some stigmatized. These assignments of meaning are relative to cultures, hence none can be considered absolute.

Pleasure and self expression are components of both spirituality and sexuality as are discipline and self transcendence.

The potential sacramentality of sex is actualized by human intention. It, like all sacramental ritual, does what it means.

Love extends human life into the infinite, "plunging it into God as a stone into the sea. Its passion and hunger cannot and should not be satisfied by the object that awakens it, for it can find its fulfilment only in 'The Whole.'"[10]

2

❧

The Sexuality of Jesus and the Human Vocation

This love is first of all fully human, that is to say, of the senses and the spirit at the same time.

Paul VI, *Humanae Vitae*

The perfecting of human love has always been recognized as a goal of religion. It is markedly so when a religion, such as Christianity, affirms the vocation to love as the primary way of identifying with the creative, redemptive, and transformative activity of the divine. Theologies of Jesus as the Christ and the Christ as God would be expected to emphasize love as the path of imitation of Christ. What is surprising is that the love modeled by the archetypal figure of Christ should emphasize the commitments of parent and neighbor to the practical exclusion of conjugal, erotic love. Of course such preferences can be explained historically. My point here is that to appeal to the life of the historical Jesus to ground such a preference is mistaken.

The humanity of Jesus, like femininity and masculinity, is constructed by us as a cultural symbol. Those things which reflect the aspirations of our own ways of being human are included; those things which incorporate the confusions and conflicts we wish to reject are left out. This need not, indeed could not be a reflective, intentional process, but nonetheless there is evidence that the affirmation "Jesus Christ is truly human" has shifting content. Its content depends on the adequacy of the anthropological assumptions that underlie its doctrinal formulation. Edward Schillebeeckx has written that our problem with developing an adequate Christology is not that we do not know enough about God, but that we do not know enough about what it means to be human.

When the classical descriptions of Jesus' manhood were formulated, it was in line with the conventional dualistic model, biased in favor of the concept of

26

rationality in Greek thought. It was unthinkable to include in normative humanity those things associated with women, connectedness, vulnerability, immersion in nature. Today a hundred-and-eighty-degree turn has been made: any formulation about the human which fails to take into account the experience of women is simply wrong: it represents not the normatively human but the male; it is vitiated because it is the partial pretending to be the universal. There is, of course, also the problem of anachronism, for each age attempts to read its own preferred values into the image of the God-man.[1] So Jesus has been cast as one of the desert hermits, as a royal ruler of the imperial kingdom, as a bishop shepherding the flock, as a divine physician healing plague-stricken victims, as a reformer cleansing old institutional forms, as the divine teacher of conventional morality, as the liberator, urging people to claim their intrinsic dignity, and of course as the supreme celibate who, free of all concupiscence, was never even tempted to intercourse with women. All of this is of course appropriate to a mythic, paradigmatic figure. Only when formulated as if it were to be taken as revelation of the full and literal God-willed way of being human, and, as such, becomes the object of faith, only then does it become oppressive. The mythic becomes pernicious when it is understood and applied literally. That many take the belief statements of the past with regard to Jesus' sexuality as literally true and absolutely founded was demonstrated dramatically, if ridiculously, when the film *The Last Temptation of Christ* was released. The presence of a sequence of scenes wherein Jesus loved and married a woman who bore his children and lived the life of a householder was widely regarded as obscene and blasphemous, even though the scenes were presented as the content of a hallucination.

The doctrine of faith, the formulated content of revelation, is that Christ is fully human and fully divine. The belief statements, written or unwritten, regarding what kind of sexual fulfillment full humanity entailed in Jesus, or in us, are subject to change. They are formulated according to historical and cultural insights and limitations, and to pretend otherwise is to mistake the words of men for the Word of God. Anyone sensitive to his own life knows that the experiences of loneliness, doubt, powerlessness, and fear have a different character when they are filtered through adult sexual awareness. To exclude on principle both this pleasure and this pain from Jesus' human life seems an impoverishment indeed. The greater impoverishment of course is ours. The precise function of the Holy Spirit, given by the risen Jesus to the community he left, was to lead that community continuously into deeper and fuller knowledge of Christ. The Spirit has only just begun to speak to the churches about the sexuality of Jesus. Why? Because just as our appreciation of his humanity is dependent on our insight into our own, so is our acceptance of his sexuality conditional upon our esteem for our own. The incarnation, in a real sense, is not complete until the community of people discovers God disclosed in their own humanity; just so, an element of Christology is lacking until we can allow ourselves to formulate images of Jesus entering as deeply into the passion of his sexuality as we have done regarding the passion of his suffering.

There have, it seems, been moments of such insight in the history of ideas. Leo Steinberg, an art historian, has defended the thesis that much Renaissance painting and sculpture, both Italian and Northern, had its inspiration in the theological thesis that Jesus assumed a humanity "complete in all its parts." The reference to "all its parts" was a way of acknowledging explicitly Jesus' sexual anatomy and thereby the unquestionable completeness of his humanity. Paintings of the infant as well as the dead and risen Christ displayed or emphasized the genitalia of Christ for the purpose of exhibiting what might otherwise be denied. The total nudity of the child in many of the paintings had become so conventional that for most of the last four hundred years the point was missed: in each of more than two hundred depictions the focal point of the paintings composition is an *ostentatio genitalium,* that is, a stylized gesture in which the mother points to the infant's genitals, the grandmother fondles them, or the adult Christ himself points to or holds them in the midst of his death agony. Besides the pointing and touching, there is unmistakable evidence of erection in the infant, the dying man and the risen God-man. Amazing to reviewers of Steinberg's book are neither the theological motivation nor the performance of the art depicting the sexual awareness and potency of Jesus. Rather what is perplexing is that the post-Renaissance religious community failed to have seen and understood the artists' intention in all these works of art. As the iconography of the East worked out in nonverbal form a theology of the divinity of Christ, so the Renaissance artists used bodily detail to flesh out a theology of his humanity. Why has it been so undeveloped in words? Denial seems the only explanation, and fear that the official Christology that from the sixteenth century had fallen into Docetist patterns should be protected from change. Further, a social system that considered the clandestine as the proper arena for sex could not easily support its explicit use as the warrant of wholeness. The Renaissance artist, frank about the sexual and unambivalent about its beauty, could celebrate the sexuality of Jesus. When the humanity of the God-man was out of theological fashion, how settle the doubt better than by calling attention to the Christ's physicality? The epiphany of the divinity may have been in the blinding light of the mountain of transfiguration, but the epiphany of Jesus' real humanity continues in the warm comfort of the genitals, ordinary like anyone else's.

A later age did not ask about the nude body: Is this true, good, or beautiful? but Is this seemly? It's the later age not the earlier that should have to justify itself. Up until the time of Rubens the erotic was entirely acceptable as the content of church art. From the nineteenth century on, the erotic has been judged unseemly for the house of God. This can, I think, be read as a statement by default about the superficiality of contemporary belief in the reality of the incarnation. The later age also asked anxiously, "Weren't they too preoccupied with sexuality?" demeaning the artists of the past by painting diapers on the cherubs and infants. It has been unable to apply one of the psychological insights of our time: shame, not acknowledgement, produces unhealthy preoccupation.

If the formula "Jesus is like us in all things save sin" is in fact understood popularly to mean he is like us in all things except sex, then the problem for a theology of sexuality and spiritual growth is at least clear. It is already commonplace to acknowledge that the Gospels do not address the issues of Jesus' personal lifestyle. Some would interpret this to mean that Jesus was not extraordinary in his sexual expression, and would even conclude that the absence of direct statements about his celibacy would point to the probability that he was indeed married for at least part of his life. The same position could claim further evidence by omission by pointing to the fact that Paul, when he was justifying his own celibate status, did not call upon the example of Jesus, which would have been significantly more persuasive than the arguments Paul finally hit upon (1 Cor. 7:7—"I say this by way of concession [to those who wanted to disregard the teaching about conjugal rights between husband and wife and the need for mutual consideration], not of command. I wish that all were as I myself am. But each has his own special gift from God, one of one kind and one of another.").[2] An obvious reason Paul would not call upon Jesus' celibacy to authorize his own and justify an admittedly dangerous lifestyle (v. 2) could be that the tradition of Jesus' celibacy derives from later devotional rather than biblical or theological sources authoritative in the early communities. Clement of Alexandria argued that the ascetics had exaggerated and misunderstood Paul's teaching, and said that although Jesus never married, he did not intend for his human followers, in this respect at least, to follow his example: "the reason that Jesus did not marry was that, in the first place, he was already engaged, so to speak, to the church; and, in the second place, he was not an ordinary man."[3] It is evident that Clement is accepting the assumptions of his day and trying to make them coherent with contemporary needs; he is certainly not questioning the assumptions regarding marriage and asceticism. Believing Paul to be the author of both the early epistles, for example, Romans and Corinthians, and the later Pastorals, for example, Timothy and Titus, he claims, as the church does generally in its exegesis, that Paul endorsed both marriage and celibacy, teaching "self-control and continence," but nowhere excluding "self-controlled marriage." Clement rejects the view held by Tatian and others that the sin of Adam and Eve was sexual intercourse. Sexual intercourse he declares to be from nature, by which he clearly meant from God. To assume Jesus was never "tempted" sexually, and that that loaded term means he never experienced desire or arousal is simply absurd. He is not only responsive to sensuous goods, including wine, but he is actually shown in the Gospels as tempted to other sins. To use the word *temptation* with regard to natural movements of sexual response to stimuli is to assume that it, the response and the stimulus, was a result of the Fall, not part of the original goodness of created man. It would be instructive about our attitudes to use the word *tempted* to describe normal desire for food. That simple linguistic exercise would show how extended, through rigorism and asceticism, had become the range of the illicit in comparison with the licit in sexual options for the good Christian, not to mention the good Christ. Of course the conventional views of Augustine and Thomas would not have allowed Jesus either erection or mastur-bation.[4] Symeon the New Theologian (d. 1022) assigns distinct functions to the members of the body of Christ conceived as a figure of the church. Among these members the "thighs" stand for "those who bear within themselves the generative power of the divine ideas of mystical theology and who give birth to the Spirit of salvation on earth."[5]

The tradition that Jesus adopted celibacy, at least after his baptism and reception of the Holy Spirit, has been read by some as indicating the influence of Essenism on Christian practice. Scholars also point out the obvious, that to argue from omission is weak. On both sides, those who assume Jesus' celibacy and those who argue for a more conventional lifestyle for his time, all that can be gathered is supposition, not fact. Any historical search for the sexuality of Jesus is doomed to failure. But the issue is not really Jesus' sexuality; that does not need proof. What is needed is a new awareness in his followers. More than textual witnesses, a credible theological way of relating the sexual with the holy is needed. That is why I would hope to highlight the fact that the humanity of Jesus, as we have it, is a symbol, and a symbol that is incomplete to the point of uselessness for human life without its fully developed sexuality.[6] A student wrote out the following question, as if to speak it aloud would be unacceptable:

> If sexuality is sacred and essential to a wholly integrated human experi-ence; if sexuality may be considered an expression of God's grace and love; and if Christ was indeed fully human, is it not appropriate to consider that perhaps Christ did not abstain from sexual activity?

After all, Jesus Christ is the point at which God and sexuality must be discussed together or forever remain separate.

VOCATION AND LIFESTYLE

The source of much of the urgency as well as the confusion on the issue of Jesus' sexuality is confusion between the notions of vocation and lifestyle. So long as the term "vocation" is used exclusively for the celibate lifestyle, a not-so-subtle demeaning of sexual activity is commonplace. By analogy, marriage, and less frequently, the chosen single life have been referred to as vocations. But that analogous use of terminology has neither cleared the confusion nor increased the sense in people of valued options. Marriage was considered in medieval times as an *officium,* an order, in the church. Vowed celibacy too is an order, that is, an institution, an endorsed and public lifestyle. These exist for the sake of the community to realize some aspect for the growth of that community. Spouses are not called to marriage, but within marriage they are called to completion of life, to union with God in co-creating, co-redeeming, and co-sanctifying activity. Priests and religious are not, precisely speaking, called to the "Evangelical" life in the sense of "Gospel living" but to the evangelical life in the sense of a life of supererogation, that is, one which commits itself to more than is required. It is within the particular definition of the lifestyle of the evangelical counsels that vowed persons are presumed to be able to find the life with God to which they feel called. The call to completion is vocation; the daily arrangements are lifestyle. Vocation is the larger category, shared by all. Jesus is paradigm of the call to fuller humanity envisioned by Christians. Jesus then is a model of vocation, not lifestyle.

The imitation of Christ, as spiritual writers have always affirmed (even though parenthetically) is compatible with every station in life and reserved to none. Adhering to the holy one, continuing to strive to be what we are called to be, "belonging to the Lord," that is what matters above all details of daily arrangements. But Jesus is not and should not be used as a literal model to be imitated in lifestyle. His "way" is to be followed, his task of taking on mankind's cause as his own is to be accepted. To live in the same way as Jesus lived means to discover for ourselves today a way of being that corresponds effectively to what Jesus' mode of existence was in his own times. He lived his life as a man for others. He loved and served, not only those it was socially acceptable to love but also the outcasts and pariahs of his society.

A lifestyle is chosen, but only within the limitations of the larger call that the person hears. They are not unconnected, for obligatory ways of living grow out of vocation. Concrete factors, unique to the person in her place and time, affect the evolution, or sometimes the invention of an appropriate lifestyle. A student reflected on the experience of life as a call.

Vocation is an overarching, heartfelt sense of call which inspires persons to participate in and contribute to the world. For example, an individual may respond to the call to love within the context of married or single life. Individuals may find that their experiences of love are most profound, most vital outside the norm of heterosexual relations and inside the realm of homosexual, bisexual, or even celibate living.

The division of the religious community into an elite which withdrew from the world in order to be free from the constraints of sexuality and the masses which remained embedded in the profane world of everyday society was one particularly brilliant historical solution to remaining on the horns of the dilemma (how relate sex to sanctity). The laity reproduced itself within the restrictions of church-supervised monogamy. The elite withdrew into celibacy and monasticism, recruiting members through "vocations" rather than through sexual interaction. Sexual activity, in theory at least, was the province of the laity. To order the irrational and destructive manifestations of sexual desire was one of the most important tasks of human social organization. But extreme forms of asceticism, some rejected as heretical, developed and continue to recur. Ironically the very increase in rigidity and numbers of rules could be read as a sign that the asexual life never successfully took hold as a viable ideal. The purification rituals of the Old Law, circumcision and food taboos, returned as taboos regarding sexual practices. But the priority of sexual control over sexual development was effectively established. The more appropriate priority, I argue here, is not that of restraint over indulgence but that of vocation over lifestyle. "First choose your path, then choose your partner," is one way the order of importance has been expressed. The fundamental option is vocation; the series of choices by which that option is lived out is lifestyle.

In terms of sexuality, the person's vocation is to develop toward full and integrated wholeness, the fruit of which is freedom, out of which one is able to have possession of oneself in order to give oneself fully to shared life. In his *Familiaris Consortio,* John Paul II wrote: "Creating the human race in his own image and continually keeping it in being, God inscribed in the humanity of man and woman the vocation, and thus the capacity and responsibility, of love and communion. Love is therefore the fundamental and innate vocation of every human being" (par. 11). We are constituted as sexual and spiritual, and in the particular mode of being human each is condition for the other. The norm and expectation, therefore the vocation of a human being, must be seen as toward sexual expressiveness. The form and frequency of the activity, the lifestyle, stands under the same sort of givens and guidelines that limit and enable all other human development within an interpersonal context. It will be virtuous insofar as it expresses and causes love and justice, peace and growth, joy and beauty, life that is centered and productive. The perception that abstinence from coitus defines the norm for Christian love, and that those who cannot accept omission as a norm are allowed sexual activity only for procreation, has lost its following. This is not to say that such limits, at certain times, for certain people, within certain situations are not appropriate. But that the normative human life is to be without sexual expression, development, or fulfillment is a failed concept.

Completion is the work of grace, and grace is capable of functioning within any natural structures. There must be a structure, but what form this structure will take depends on what best does the opening, the surprising, the healing at a given time. Can anyone dictate in the abstract what is the best structure for a couple in love during wartime? for refugees separated for decades from legal spouses? for lesbian women? for an incest survivor who is a single parent with a deep suspicion of men?

Consequent upon progress in the vocation to grow sexually, one does have choices between good and evil. They are choices of how and in what pattern of human relationships a person's development toward wholeness, in this real situation in which he finds himself, can best proceed. Where the individual person experiences greater coinherence with the Spirit, there lifestyle choices would be discerned as better, but better in degree not in kind, and better for the individual not for humankind. The optimum relationship for men and women in any cultural epoch must be that which best keeps them open to God's healing and saving entry into their lives. For most women, for most of history, the choice, assumed to be inevitable, between a serious spiritual and sexual life, meant acquiescence to their reproductive destiny and the internalization of the false notion that they belonged more to the flesh than the spirit, more to the husband who needed their services than to the holy God whose image they embodied. Now the revolution is entering its second, long overdue phase, when women, with a sense of the sacredness of their sexuality, claim rightful place in the sphere of Spirit.

The traditional teaching on law and grace is in keeping with the order of this dynamic. It is not the renunciatory lifestyle that produces grace, but the response to grace that takes forms sometimes of detachment and sometimes of attachment. In the history of spirituality, perhaps because it was largely written or censored by men, perhaps because of the exegetical tradition, letting go, detachment, has been interpreted to have greater intrinsic value. But the movements of the Spirit toward embodiment, engagement, of taking hold are the fruit equally of grace. Neither embracing nor renouncing sexual pleasure is in itself a state to be preferred. Both are necessary phases in the dynamic of a responsive individual or institution.

A young lesbian woman, speaking to a group about the dilemma in which she lived, being Catholic in a committed lesbian relationship, cut through it all with the clarity of her evaluation: "I tried religious life at one time, but I had to leave. My experience of God comes much more strongly through human love." When lifestyle and vocation are in step, confidence glows; life is luminous.

Discernment

Discernment, a skill intensified as a gift, is important for people trying to make good faith choices regarding lifestyle. Whatever its content, a lifestyle conducive to spiritual growth will be characterized by a number of qualities, including progress toward personal freedom, increased capacity for intimacy, and an environment in which ecstasy is possible.

Progress toward personal freedom might be recognized, not so much by autonomy as by interdependence. Its opposite is addictive behavior, sometimes described in psychological terms as compulsion or obsession. The scriptural reference might be Paul's declaration against excessive dependence on the Law: "For God has called us to peace. Only let every one lead the life which the Lord has assigned to him, and in which God has called him: (1 Cor. 7:15, 17). This is the effective spiritual criterion that has led many a woman to reject a previous lifestyle, for example, a patriarchal marriage in which roles of domination and submission were lived out, for an autonomous lifestyle.

> The single most important life experience concerning my sexuality was when I admitted to myself how unhappy I was sexually and made the decision to work through my fears and rage in hopes of finding a sexuality of my own. This was a huge decision for my life. I separated from the man I had desperately committed myself to when I was fourteen, I lost friends that couldn't understand what I was doing and I enraged my family for not going along with what has been expected. . . . Happily, I am learning what feels healthy and right for me sexually, I have choices.

Whatever its difficulties, including loss of financial support and spousal companionship, divorce has been perceived by some as a move that is necessary for the salvation of their personhood, their "souls." A significant number of men have also invoked this criterion to leave the celibate lifestyle required by the Roman Catholic priesthood to carry out what they recognized to be larger vocations as human beings. Leaps of faith and steps in spiritual progress are made daily by men and women who change jobs, professions, habits ingrained over long periods of time, because they recognize in them a bondage that prevents integration and full self-possession. There is some evidence that, in our time, the preoccupation with sex that takes people away from their vocation to wholeness is more the result of false guilt, poor self-understanding and self-acceptance, artificial stimulation through media images and general lack of balance in the ordering of life than it is of intentional bodily expression of excess sexual passion. The use of sex is a relative value; the lack of use of sex is a relative value. Neither is to have power over the person. Both are powers of the person. These are lifestyle choices within the absolute (though ambiguous) mandate of the vocation to human becoming. Yet in the performance of the sexual choices of daily life, I reveal more than this or that particular and relative thing about my lifestyle. In choices, such as who and how to touch, where and with whom to be intimate, when and why to refuse the gift of presence, I create connections with the Absolute. More than my way of being teacher, lover, aunt is at stake. What is actually composed day by day is myself as a person in entirety, a vocation. At the same time as I know pleasure in a friend, there is ecstasy in the Spirit; my being there for my students is a performance also of my "belonging to Christ"; and while having fun with nieces and nephews, I know what it is to play in the sight of the Lord of the universe. My vocation is a robe woven by way of my lifestyle; I am not called out of my lifestyle into a vocation.

In a Christian theology of the discernment of a call there are a number of elements. The person always has some sort of inner experience of call. Practically speaking this might be no more than an internalized sense of one's religious or spiritual identity. For Christian theology, it is an inner experience decisively begun in the externally visible event of baptism, explicitly affirmed as having taken hold in confirmation, and continually deepened and integrated into daily life through frequent liturgical celebration of the eucharist. For once-born personalities, to use the intriguing concept formulated by William James,[7] there may be no single dramatic moment associated with the experience of inner call, but it is known nonetheless to be real when reclaimed reflectively. For twice-born personalities, the call, as well as the experiences of infidelity and reconciliation to it, may be quite dramatic. Stories of conversion are stories of vocation recognized. When those stories can be told, a milestone has been reached in the spiritual life.

In addition to the inner experience of call, a theology of discernment requires objective evidence that the person has the ability to meet its practical demands. A "call" can be tracked as a continuous line between the divine energy and this particular individual, but the fulfillment of the call requires human credibility. Joan of Arc was able to complete what she perceived to be asked of her by God's voices also because she had considerable military genius and was able to gain credibility with the troops she was called to lead. We are called within our personal situation to a human way of being. Whoever wants to affirm the accuracy of their inner sense of call, must look to what is given in their intelligence, character, circumstances, opportunities, as verified by someone outside themselves. I can be absolutely sure I am not called to parenthood in a physical sense if I am physically incapable of conceiving or carrying a fetus to term. Not my natural limitations but my tendency to settle for less than I can achieve when enhanced by the Spirit are transcended in the notion of vocation. The Spirit drives out fear, self-hatred, small-mindedness, narcissism. I may not always know at the outset what is attainable from what is beyond me, but that only serves to reemphasize the point: only that can be required of me for which I have the necessary qualities and conditions.

A third point in the theology of vocation insists that the specification of the call be affirmed by others in the community. Some kind of credentialing, formal or informal, through ritual or by the literal undergoing of transformation through illness or trauma is likely always to be associated with the discernment of vocation. Here emerges one of the crucial points in human development. The peculiar inequities of vision and power have produced situations in which only some within the human community are presumed capable of a spiritual life. The greatest sin against our own sexuality and that of others has been the blindness which has prevented us in general and the lack of love which has prevented us in particular from affirming in each other the call to love God by becoming as fully loving sexual human beings as possible. The inexplicability of it all is demonstrated through a number of institutional power issues.

For no apparent good reason, many Catholics are left for years "outside the church" because of a second marriage after divorce, which the official community did not recognize, in fact which it condemned as living in sin. For easily apparent poor reasons, marginalized groups have been rejected even from the act of worship because their sexual orientation or practice was considered deviant, among them gay men and lesbian women, divorced and remarried persons, those who support women's responsible ownership of their own reproductive capacity, especially if they are politically active for a pro-choice position. If persons, Christian or otherwise, do not live their sexual lives as vocation, it is at least partly due to the lack of this third requirement: they have not been called by the community to do so; moreover, in some instances they have been actively prevented from so doing.

Intimacy

A second criterion by which any lifestyle could be measured as compatible with vocation is intimacy. The capacity for intimacy, which I will define as the experience of being wholly and deeply touched by others, is a mark of maturity and a fruit of the Spirit. It involves an awareness of one's own depths, along with the recognition that feelings are not in themselves suspect. Feelings are always good, always to be accepted as normal. Acceptance of feelings enables a person to be intimate with herself in moments of solitude. Otherwise, she tends to become anonymous to herself, to have no inner life.

> I have been monogamous all my life, but have achieved intimacy only when I was willing to risk sharing my emotions and only when the man I was with was willing to accept me and also willing to share himself. . . . I don't believe that most people open themselves up to each other the first time they meet. The experience didn't happen to me until a time when I was comfortable enough with myself to be myself and to share that person with someone else. When I learned to accept and love the person I am, I could be that person with someone else without fear of rejection. I could go into a relationship saying in effect, this is who I am. If you like who I am that's fine; and if you don't, that's fine, too. In former relationships my partner and I didn't seem to be able to allow each other the time to explore and discover ourselves. There's a certain amount of self-awareness that can only be learned over a period of time, I believe. Some people are able to learn and grow together and some aren't.

Those who deny their bodies and their feelings, thinking that the real self is the mental subject, are never wholly available. Some part, the vital, spontaneous part, is always under constraint. Touch is always feared. An aspect of mystery, interpersonal mystery, is forever closed to them because it is revealed through reciprocal attention to our male and female bodies. This absence from one's own emotional self has been called repression. As a habitual state of being, it has consequences not just for self-intimacy but for shared intimacy.[8] Repressed persons must avoid personal situations, for such situations always hold the possibility of a tender moment, and tenderness leads to danger. They anxiously scan the social horizon to insure that no one violates their sacred space. They are intolerant of the intimacies of others even as they revel in seeking them out for condemnation. They glare at sexual expressions but do not permit themselves to see anything that expresses human sexuality positively. They are alienated and hostile to play and self-expression. Insisting on governing all relationships, they fall into considering "illicit" those which they themselves have not permitted. How absurd this can become was illustrated recently by the director of a Center for Fitness and Wholistic Living who questioned a group for going on an "unauthorized" hike. Repressed persons are especially dangerous in positions of authority. For many cultures, the capacity for intimacy is a mark of mature leadership. It might well become a key indicator for readiness for religious or political candidates for leadership at this time in the technologically developed cultures when know-how is less rare than relatedness. No one skill or structure, including a monogamous relationship, is able to guarantee intimacy. It is developed more than chosen, and its presence in a person's relationships is more a sign of the stage of development of the persons involved than a function of a particular framework.

Ecstasy

As important as intimacy to test the rightness of a lifestyle, so is the availability of moments of ecstasy. Excitement, adventure, being beside oneself with feeling are not luxuries but are the essential integrators of human life. Ecstasy is the experience of the temporary dissolution of boundaries. The moment, and it is always momentary, is one in which some otherwise distant reality is glimpsed as here and now, one with oneself. The "unitive glimpse" is capable of completely reorganizing a life, a fact to which the accomplishments of many a mystic point. More often, we hear about the accomplishments but are unaware of the ecstatic moments at their source, until allowed through an autobiography or journal to gain insight into a process that is always creative and revolutionary. But the ecstatic moment recreates the personality as well as introducing new insights, inventions, and lives into the universe. When the boundaries re-form, it is never with quite the same configuration as before. Scientists concerned to understand the chemistry and motivation of human drug use tell us that it is not only human beings who experience, indeed create situations in which they can experience, an altered state of consciousness. There is no mammal who does not try by some means, physical or chemical, to alter its state of consciousness. Small animals twirl around in circles or mimic attack and escape patterns, presumably to stimulate release of varying levels of drive chemistry. The command center in the human brain, known as the hypothalamus, releases varying levels of epinephrine (once called adrenalin); dopamine, a very powerful pleasure substance; endorphins, recently discovered reward substances; and serotonin, a substance associated with sleep or rest. These natural biochemicals can be mimicked by the use of alcohol, heroin, opiates, and various depressants or stimulants. Research has shown that it is probable that the hypothalamus is suggestible and programmable. This only confirms empirically what religious liturgies have always understood intuitively and incorporated into worship. Current research suggests that chemical dependency and eating disorders are the result of a drive process gone awry. This happens when a substance (alcohol, drugs, food) begins to mimic natural reward, and reward reshapes the drive. During the process of romantic love, the substance phenylethylamine has been discovered in human beings. Sex is rewarded by dopamine, norepinephrine, and endorphins which produce powerful pleasure rewards after sex. In a similar way, but with a different intensity, serotonin and other biochemical elements may reward rest, also called sexual "afterglow." These behaviors are reinforced by the command center and are necessary for the continuation of life and the human species.[9] Therefore it is suggested by some researchers that so-called sexual addiction, like chemical addiction or eating disorders, is a drive process in disarray. Individuals who abstain from one mood altering substance which might in fact mimic the natural biochemicals the body produces may seek a similar mood altered state produced biochemically through sex. In such a theory it is not the substance (sex, food, alcohol) addicted individuals are dependent upon, but they are dependent physically and psychologically on the mood altered state provided by the biochemicals released in the human body during the sex act. Further research may ultimately provide additional answers to managing the body's ability to provide altered states of consciousness. For this consideration of sexuality and spirituality, it is already clear that here is something that is clearly symbolic of the unity of body and mind. Persons' freedom with regard to ecstatic experience in relation to their overall well-being is a spiritual concern. Compulsions destroy lives. With accurate information, with growth toward the ability to make and live with choices, and with the support of an involved community, individuals can ultimately be empowered to choose to cease behaviors that may be causing harm in their lives. But never should the specter of abuse and addiction in particular lives overshadow the promise of ecstasy in a union based on the joy of free and mutual love. When genital feelings are properly cultivated, tenderness, lived out as respectful affection, can be the transforming and exhilarating result. For adults, genital feelings are a primary source of ecstatic experiences. Intellectual, aesthetic, and religious intimations of union are also part of a full human life. Any lifestyle that is so constituted as to prevent peak experiences, one that fits so poorly that in it an individual has no room to know the excitement of newness, leaves little room for spiritual growth.

IDENTITY AND ROLE

In addition to assumptions about Jesus' sexuality and confusions about vocation and lifestyle, I think assumptions about gender role get in the way of spiritual growth for many people. Gender has been made political to an extraordinary degree in our time. With the forming of alliances comes resentment and anger, sometimes veiled, but always significant for the process of learning to love. Sexual identity and gender role refer to aspects of the human being's development to normal adulthood. The term sexual identity refers to the fact that identity as a male or female is assigned to an individual as possessing male or female genital organs. When persons speak of crises in the development of "sexual identity," they are, however, often alluding to concerns, not about being male or female, but about being sexually attracted to the same or opposite sex. Strictly speaking, one's sexual identity is not in terms of being heterosexual or homosexual. Those designations are of very recent usage. One's sexual identity is in terms of being male or female. In contrast to the anatomical determination of sexual identity, gender role as masculine or feminine is much more ambiguous, being the product of cultural conditioning, family patterns, and the religious sacralization of particular characteristics or values. While it is obvious that a functioning adult needs a clear sense of gender role (What is it for me to be a valued and effective woman?), it is equally obvious in our time that an overly restrictive separation of roles between males and females and a too-complete identification of the person with her approved role can stand in the way of personal, social, professional, and spiritual development.

The issue that gender raises is not how men and women are different in responding to things, nor is it how similar they are. The real issue is: How do both men and women achieve sexual personal wholeness in a situation of disparity of power between them?

The social construction of gender specifies, in practical ways, who the person will be. It is adopted as personal agenda: I am a girl; I am a boy. While anatomy is given, gender is both task and destiny. Strangely, biology and anatomy are far more open to individual peculiarities. Sexual viability, bodily diversity are so scary that they have been channeled into certain routine patterns. Conformity with these maintains social stability because ambiguity in the interpretation of signals is reduced and expectations can be developed and met with a minimum of individual care for communication.

Masculinity

Are there forms of masculinity which can be chosen which are not directly organized around domination?[10] Is the concept of masculinity as powerful only viable when paired with the active social subordination of women? Is the one to be the price of the other? If this is what is signified by complementarity, then it is closer to conspiracy than to cooperation. On principal, when inequality sustains a necessary institution, such as, allegedly, the family, is it less unjust? If autonomy were affirmed as a value for all and incorporated into feminine style, more creative social structures might develop. Moreover men's dependency could express itself in ways more conducive to intimacy than to self-contempt.

The complexity of gender issues should not mask the fact that they involve opportunity for the exercise of freedom and responsibility. At the least one is responsible for one's own decisions about whether to participate or not.

Men who have heard and accepted the feminist critique of the systematic subordination of women can be overtaken by guilt. The desire for redemption has led to the formation of men's groups in which they work on recognizing and changing their own and others' sexist attitudes and behavior toward women. In such groups and perhaps by individual men's choice of professions, they work at understanding their own masculinity, how it was formed in growing up, and how it constricts the expression of their emotions and limits the depth of their relationships; and they provide emotional support to each other. The tendency among some is to become uncritically "feminist." But this may be just as inauthentic as any masculinist denial that inequality exists. It makes no sense for a person to take responsibility for, and feel guilt about what the other adult people do or have done in the past. Moral agency means to take responsibility for what I myself do and for its consequences. These of course include how personal actions either sustain or subvert the continuation of structures of oppression. But to take responsibility for, and feel guilt about, those structures as a whole is at one level paranoid, at another paralyzing. Anger among women who were late-comers to consciousness of their own oppression can be equally self-defeating, until they understand that anger is energy and can be channeled to action in ways that guilt cannot.

Another approach taken by some men faced with the uncomfortable fact of the disparity of power between the sexes was to claim that men are equally oppressed. If a woman's sex role oppresses her, so does a man's sex role. One response was to try, through retreats, encounter groups, and one-to-one counselling, to break out of the stereotypes and repair the psychic and spiritual damage they caused. The oppression of women is then treated as an illusion or an excess of role rigidity among women themselves. Homosexuality is ignored; guilt is treated as irrational or obsolete. The main thing to be overcome is men's emotional inhibition. The effect of such a point of view, according to one researcher, is to leave inequality uncontested and simply to update heterosexual masculinity. Some efforts to update theology, through the work of male theologians convinced of *part* of the feminist agenda, might serve as an unusual example of this inadequate response. Such an approach would cooperate in revising God-language so that the Father God is endowed with characteristics of compassion and mercy formerly exclusively identified with feminine stereotypes. God's image is upgraded to that of a better male, but still male. This approach may make men feel better about being the exclusive holders of power, once that power has been challenged, but it does nothing to challenge the institutional arrangements that produce the disparity in power.

Today, in the midst of conflicted gender relations, children are being introduced into a situation in which more aggressive, dominant, and violent models of masculinity are being actively constructed for adolescents. At the same time, many single female parents, wary of the kind of masculinity which left them hurt and abandoned, are raising their sons as women-defined men. Some observers would say that it is not so much an exaggerated "macho" interpretation of the male role that accounts for the high levels of violence against women as it is insecurity and lack of adequate models, after all, the reconstruction of male roles lags behind the reform of roles for women. The increasing marginalization of men from the family can be documented. Women (and perhaps the media) have concluded that men have failed as husbands and fathers. Some are basically disillusioned with men, are familiar with the feminist arguments about men's unjustified privileges, and systematically support each other against the men who are their supervisors and managers. If men have not accepted that opinion of themselves, they are at least aware that a particular image of the role of men is under seige.

Femininity

A woman's social self has been created for her, not just symbolically but also physically within the stereotypical feminine gender role. She puts on femininity with her clothes and manners in such a way that it changes the very shape her body occupies in space. Femininity in a sense takes up residence in her, as is all the more evident as it changes with the stages of life or with shifts of fashion. Femininity is perceived to be particularly "plastic" as hair, dress, makeup trends claim her adherence. It is not easy for her to ignore signs of that allegiance, for the standards are fickle, changing as if to test her malleability. Even as the woman of today prides herself on being "unladylike" according to the standards of yesterday, she is conforming to the standards of today.

Even such an apparently unchangeable characteristic as size is at issue. More than her supposed independence, brashness, or sexual liberation, the typical American woman's height contributes to her reputation in the international community for a lack of femininity.

> Once on a crowded subway car in Tokyo I felt at the outer limits of appropriate size, in peril of being a rude affront to all Japanese men and a gross insult to their country's sense of exquisite proportion. It was hardly my fault that Americans in general are a taller people, but I did not want to seem unfeminine—outsize, overbearing, impolite.[11]

When such an anomaly as women taller than most men in the world has been produced by nature, ways to compensate are developed by society. Although Lady Diana Spenser was only a half-inch shorter than Prince Charles when she wore her flat heels, she was shown to be a full head shorter on the postage stamp that commemorated their royal wedding. Anthropologist Sarah

Hrdy observed that in primate studies only those groups of gorillas and baboons in which the female is relatively as large as the male exhibit cooperative rather than male-dominant behavior. She suggested on one occasion that physical evolution may have more to say about the future of equality between men and women than feminist politics, philosophy, or ethics. When I tell my women students this, they laugh, but they continue on their diets, and sometimes their anorexic regimens by which their woman-shaped bodies are kept, at least temporarily, thin and boylike. The motivation bears some reflection. As Brownmiller expresses it,

> "I am too competitive to stand by and watch my middle thicken while other women parade their thinness like an Olympic medal. Dieting is the chief form of competition among women today, at least upwardly mobile women who strive to perfect the feminine illusion as they strive in other ways to achieve success."[11]

Because size is a problem, so is food. At the same time as fat creates the softness and curves of womanhood, it also constitutes massiveness, disgusting in her because associated with masculine bigness and power. The struggle which keeps the spiritual woman in a self-conscious relationship with her body is more a threat to her spiritual freedom than all pleasure of food or sex could be. In spite of the fact that women's bodies show a wide degree of difference in the shapes they take from their own genetic makeup as well as from childbearing and aging, it is no news that most cultures have sought, through constricting devices from corsets to surgery, to impose a preapproved, uniform shape.

Then, of course, there is the ever-present concern with hair. Barbara Walters advises the woman who is facing a challenge of any kind to "get her hair done." Why it should improve one's performance as an interviewer remains elusive until the point is grasped. Without her hair meeting the social standard, she is not fully constituted as a person who can expect (or expect herself) to succeed. The moral and religious significance of hair is a topic to be found in both Scriptures, Hebrew (Samson whose strength was cut off with his hair by the cunning of a woman; Absalom who was at the mercy of King David when his long hair caught in a tree branch and prevented his escape) and Christian (the penitent woman who dries Jesus' feet with it; the allegation of the unnaturalness of long hair on men and short hair on women; the admonition that women should cover their heads at worship because nature teaches it). Throughout history women were expected to seduce with it, endured the sculpting and perming of it, occasionally could make a little money selling it, but were never satisfied with it. Mothers and husbands determined how it should be worn (Mother: Get your hair cut; it looks witchy! Daughter: But *he* likes it long!). And if male partners do not notice even subtle changes in how it has been "done," their love is not to be trusted. Of course the greatest sign of contradiction is that while women's hair can never be too luxuriant, the other areas endowed by nature with hair, legs, underarms, even pubic hair, if it competes with the latest in swimsuit fashions, must be removed if one is not to overturn very seriously a social requirement of being feminine. Like other aspects of bodiliness, a symbol by which conformity or rebellion can be achieved with little cost and no violence, hair too reflects our spiritual conflicts.

The peculiarly complicated quality of women's clothes is one of the first impressions of the young girl who has entered with puberty the social requirement new to her—to be a "Girl." Suddenly, or so it seems to the girl herself, the abundance of healthy activity associated with vitality is now suspect. No longer is being a tomboy rewarded. Probably somewhere around the time of the first formal dance or Miss Teen contest, female onlookers are jolted with the realization that femininity is literally "worn." If you do it often enough a process seems natural; but the gap between functional dress and women's ritual garb is too great for evolution. This is impersonation. In Brownmiller's apt phrase, all women and some men are female impersonators. That being feminine requires acting is not surprising; taking on any role engages acting ability. What is remarkable, to men and women alike, is that femininity can be put on in such an external way. It is not just a problem of social life making girls grow up too fast, so that form precedes function; it is that no matter how old they would get, they would never grow naturally into this packaged commodity. Feminine clothes which neither protect the body nor facilitate its free movement have only one function: constraint from actions that are forthright and self-assertive, that would violate the rules of male-female relations. The neck ring may be elegant and expensive, and the footwear flattering; women may wear the frills proudly but the spiritual significance for those who can see is the achievement of another successful subordination. Once more a potential center of action has accepted reduction to an object of admiration. The gender role wears the woman proudly.

A young woman wrote:

> I hate to be pessimistic but there seem to be so many anxieties that go along with being female. One of the most obvious anxieties is appearance, and for me the most obvious case was my mother. She has always struck me as being a remarkably attractive woman. I marvel even now at how well she looks compared to the other women in her thirtieth high school reunion picture, and how fancy. I am also amazed at how much time, energy and effort she invests in her appearance. It is bad enough to have to wear a dress, but to try on four . . . and then, all the

make up. It sometimes seems to me that my mother's most characteristic remark about me, which I have heard thousands of times is, "That is real nice, dear, but maybe a little blush." She was and is recognized as being pretty, but it has sometimes seemed that that is all.

In spite of the harshness of that judgment, the accessories of a constructed femininity are not necessarily to be rejected. The history of symbols has shown that the same things and actions can be given and in turn impart completely new meanings. It is not the clothes which makes the woman; it is the spiritually aware and free women of present and future who will choose which of the concrete signs of past femininity are to remain and be transformed and which are to be left behind. A mark of such freedom is the ability to move in and out of particular roles, knowing oneself to be more than what is given in an especially riveting performance.

It is undeniable that femininity, in spite of its artificialities, has been declared natural in a way that masculinity has not. It has been opposed to culture, thus given moral weight and burdened with assumptions of its immutability. But gender roles have never been innate; they have always been learned, even though they have been successfully marketed as natural because linked to biological roles in reproduction. A common argument against more flexibility in roles considered appropriate to men and women is the concern that this would threaten family stability. When femininity is defined solely in relation to childcare and domestic work, and where "the family" is the only sphere in which women have any power, the diminishment of that role is feared. It is a common response in crisis to play upon the fear of losing what one already has. In terms of gender, lessening the inflexibility of roles would represent a gain in personal spiritual power, a gain in choices and self-knowledge. Increased flexibility is frightening as all freedom is frightening for those not prepared to set their own goals. The question raised by gender is that of the tension between the values of autonomy and relationality. Is the social construction of the feminine just another way of being freely human, to be chosen with integrity as the outer expression of one's inner subjectivity? Is it appropriate to being a moral agent? Or is it in fact being offered, in a way that cannot be declined, the role of object? Cast forever as Other (in Simone de Beauvoir's classical expression), is the suppression of her liberty required by the role? To accept it under such conditions would be bad faith. Does accepting femininity as one's way of being signal the internalization of oppression that Gerda Lerner so clearly analyzed? Is such a woman co-opted into the role of her own oppressor, whether for protection, self-worth, or security? This would entangle her in an unwinnable conflict because she would be pitted against her own growth. And here we return to the crucial question: How can women and men be authentically feminine and masculine in a situation of such disparity of power? My analysis does not resolve the conflict, but recognizes that it is of the order of Spirit. What is at stake is not just the stability of families but the salvation of persons. The challenge is not just for a femininity compatible with adult autonomy; it is also a call for unconventional masculinity and creative forms of family living.

Traditional gender constructions, then, both for women and men, are in a period of dismantling. After gender breakdown reconstruction will have to take place. The spiritual opportunity it offers our society is great. What values will influence the new forms that must evolve? Faced with just such a question, a number of women responded to a survey as follows. [12] They want:

1. In relation to work
   a) In the family: control of the household budget, more equal sharing of housework, an independent wage for women with the right to spend it
   b) In the workplace: freedom from sexual harassment
2. In relation to power
   a) In the family: control over decisions about the children, personal independence which includes freedom from physical or emotional abuse by husbands and male friends
   b) In the workplace: freedom from arbitrary authority, being taken seriously by unions, professional organizations, and other forms of solidarity which increase power
3. In relation to sexuality
   a) In the family: adequate contraception which clearly signals control of one's reproductive power, as well as one's sexuality; the right of teenagers to be sexual beings and to be active in initiating and controlling sexual experiences; the right of married women to set terms with husbands or leave unsatisfying marriages; the right of never married, divorced, and widowed women to be active in initiating and controlling sexual encounters
   b) In the workplace: freedom to refuse and initiate sexual encounters, freedom from gender stereotypes

Are these in any sense spiritual values? Religious authorities, who once could command obedience on what was salvational in matters of gender, no longer have the credibility to arbitrate those questions. But was it a matter of spiritual growth just because it was seen as virtuous obedience? In some ways obedience is still exacted. Only now it is doctors, therapists, and scientists who have succeeded the clergy in dominance. The medicalization of sexual "shoulds" has been traced by a number of historians, notably, Barbara Ehrenreich and

Deirdre English on the medicalization of women's bodies in the United States and Vern and Bonnie Bullough on the remaking of sexual myth. A medical theory of sexual life has been accompanied by an expectation of control as hormonal replacement; surgical procedures for conception, birth, and conception control; and medications capable of affecting sexual appetite and potency have been prescribed. The shift from religion to medicine disguises the fact of sexuality's control by the masculine power structure by basing it on the authority of a profession that just happens to be male-dominated. Medicine has actually adopted the language of the hierarchical churches in talking about "lay" people, and contrasting their ignorance and errors with the sound judgment of the professionals. Obedience is increasingly risky as a way to spiritual and sexual health.

I think the spiritual issue at stake in gender relations is *reconciliation*. In practice, women have not found it easy to reject femininity yet value womanhood. Men have found it difficult to separate appropriate male power from the overbearing forms it may take. A certain playfulness about gender, a rejection and reordering of elements, belongs to the stage of transition. It follows a very real break with the past and carries the sense of being an outsider, which for some people makes the solution worse than the problem. In most cases where energy is high, it has gone into renegotiating relationships between women and men whose consciousness has been raised. This process of forgiveness and renewal typically takes place privately in individual sexual relationships and households. On this point there has been little exchange of ideas or experience in the public or religious arenas. When there is, it will chart a development of the spirit. There are historical moments when the possibilities of overall transformation of consciousness and culture depend more crucially on the dynamic of gender relations than on any other social force. It can be argued that we are in such a moment now.

Relations between men and women are open to transformation because they also include love, an attitude that is compatible with conflict but includes an agenda for betterment. Love is a commitment that is formative in its own way, with ramifications for the subjects' life histories. Love can change an original relationship in ways not predictable and sometimes hardly recognizable. Can love co-exist with injustice? Of course. Shulamith Firestone has in fact defined "romantic love" as the corrupted version of love that develops when the parties are unequal. Can love overturn injustice? Alice Walker in *The Color Purple* suggests that love is impossible except between equals and equality is only possible within gender, not across genders. I would want to debate that assumption, but not the assertion that love and subordination, like love and conflict, can be connected. Love alone does not redeem gender relations from dominance-subordination patterns. That is obvious. Traditional marriage, more than romantic love, systematically incorporated a loving woman into a loved man's projects, thus exempting her from launching her own projects in the world. As a student put it:

> The difficulties that come from trying to change these roles (I am overinvolved in the chaos of family life, while he sits on the sidelines) suggest that our early experiences with separation and unity are present here also. He can isolate and separate himself while being physically present. His rigid boundaries enable him to shut out the world, while I can not. He works at the expense of the family, and she works for the family at the expense of her own self.

While love can coincide with this contradiction, it is still the greatest challenger to the status quo between the genders, precisely because of its revolutionary erotic power. Parental love is not feared by the conservative, but *eros*, a force difficult to control, which breaks through old barriers, is greatly feared. Even in the form of thoughts, erotic impulses have been considered so headstrong that they should be fled rather than faced or fought. Yet, in this, eros is not unlike the Spirit who blows where she will, more likely to appear in forms that are alien and monstrous than those that conform to the expectations of the time. *Caritas*, in its stabilizing tendency, reflects the impetus to sacralization; *eros*, in its revolutionary capacity, reflects prophetic spirit. This is a permanent tension, one that can serve structural change and social transformation. To embrace both is to opt for the integration of love, to take on the spiritual task of liberation. Much of the beauty in our culture has been generated around gender relations. The bond produced by dependency is strong. It remains to see what men and women will produce as equals.

FOCAL POINTS:

Jesus' sexuality, like ours, is integral to his humanity. To ignore or deny it is to miss the opportunity to follow his body-affirming spirituality. It is to render him opaque as a revelation of what it means to be human.

Vocation is the call heard within persons' deepest being to grow toward personal wholeness and integration, participating in and contributing to the world; lifestyle is the particular and perhaps unique material and relational arrangements through which one lives out that vocation.

The complexities of gender conflict in an age of transition offer opportunities for spiritual growth. Women need men to help them toward autonomy so that they can help men toward interdependence. The spiritual issue between men and women is one of active reconciliation, a ministry in which sexuality is powerful.

3

❧

Stages in Sexual-Spiritual Growth

In the design of God, every man {sic} is called upon to develop and fulfill himself, for life is a vocation. . . . Endowed with intelligence and freedom, he is responsible for his fulfillment as for his salvation.

Paul VI, *Populorum Progressio*

Most people fail in the art of living not because they are inherently bad, or so without will that they cannot lead a better life; they fail because they do not wake up and see when they stand at the fork in the road and have to decide.

Erich Fromm

A view of spirituality as progress toward maturity is characteristic of the New Testament. Images of movement and pilgrimage, exile and homecoming have characterized its history, and more than a few have written of the spiritual "quest" in terms of going somewhere that one has never been but is recognized in the arriving as home. These are of course only images, perhaps envisioned in so linear a fashion because the writers have been proceeding from a model of initiation and hero's journey of conquest. The emphasis could just as well be on inner peace and harmony, on the model of settlers and weavers, as on trekkers and pilgrims. Whatever image were chosen, it would have to acknowledge that there is a dynamic, a movement involved, which will be represented here in the use of the language of stages. I do not propose a definable norm which all are expected to reach, or attempt to describe a chronology that links a particular stage with age. The key notion is that growth is sequential in steps that are to some extent predictable. The aim of the growth process of the

49

Christian life was formulated by the author of the letter to the Ephesians (4:13) as "so that we shall reach perfect personhood, that maturity which is proportioned to the complete growth of Christ." The diversity among people and their circumstances makes one pause, aware of the symbolic character of these religious images of progress. I only choose to venture into the language of orderly development because a model, if used intelligently and flexibly, can be an aid to self-knowledge, self-acceptance, and self-transcendence. If used unintelligently, it will produce only anxiety. Since readers of this book would have already put it down if they were looking for a formula and a quick fix, I shall overcome my hesitation and continue.

Our lives are shaped in decisive ways by our sexual histories. The form our spiritual struggle takes is in many ways determined by this sexual investment already made. Will the spiritual odyssey take the form of self-denial? meditation? reliance upon a community? friendship with a spiritual mentor? teaching? action? prophecy? suffering and sacrifice? play? Will it resemble the evolution of the "once-born" or the dramatic conversions of the "twice-born"? Will it tell a tale of affirmation or negation? Will it speak of the nearness of God or of God's absence? Our stories of sexual awakening may hold the key.

It was one of the many Christmas cap-gun fights in my cousin's basement. I was so excited about being partners with my cousin whom I idolized. He was the big 18. I was so honored when he asked me to share a secret until I found out what the secret was, and what I was supposed to do with it. It did more than change the way I felt about penises, and cap-guns, it also changed the way I felt about boys. This aspect about being female had never occurred to me before. Sure I worried about having to wear a dress or putting my bra on straight, but never before did I have to worry about being me, a girl. It not only left me with an anxiety about myself but also with a general mistrust for people.

*　　*　　*

As a child I was viewed as the property of my parents. Living in poverty, my family had few options when it came to basics concerning living conditions, health service, child-care, and education. I believe this all had an effect and is part to blame for the hard time I have had in being a sexually healthy adult woman. One major life experience helps to clarify this point. When I was five, I was sexually abused by a doctor during a required kindergarten check-up. Because of the way our society views the poor, they/we rarely complained. My mother didn't complain about the wait or the fact that the one doctor available to her children was unfit to practice medicine. Later, long after I blocked this abuse, I held on to the belief that my body was not mine to choose how and by whom I wanted it touched. Our society taught me as a female child of poverty I had no choices around my sexuality. I learned I could do what was expected and leave my body and sexuality to others.

* * *

As a child, my body was truly mine. I remember having a sense of freedom when I was three or four that I will most likely never have again. I loved my body and myself and was quite unashamed. Running naked on the beach was no big deal, and sitting in the tub with my brother never got a second thought. When I was happy I gave hugs, when I was hurting I asked for a kiss or a backrub.

STAGE ONE:
SEXUAL UNFOLDING-SPIRITUAL AWAKENING

The beginnings of sexual awareness, though often spoken of in thinglike terms as if puberty were a train that arrives at a prearranged station, are personal events dependent on interpretation. Experience is not what happens to us but what we make of what happens to us. For puberty to be a passage, an initiation, even a spiritual awakening, a communal or public meaning of it as such must be available to young people. One's own sexuality may or may not be discovered in puberty. People spend important times during later stages of their lives understanding what has already happened. When puberty is welcomed as something gratuitous, surprising, not adequately explained by the twelve or so years that went before, the personality unfolds with the sexual potency. If awareness is forced prematurely by early sexual abuse, or resisted as gross and shameful, the personality shrinks from the reality it might celebrate. The complex of feelings, physical changes, and contradictory attitudes is characteristic of adolescent development.

The happy child in the third story above, continues as follows:

I believe that it was junior high or fifth grade, right at the onset of menstruation, that I began to be ashamed. More and more I wanted to hide my body and cover up the fact that it was changing rapidly. I was embarrassed and confused and I coped with this turmoil by trying to stay a child and conceal my ever-nearing womanhood. For the same reasons I became suspicious of touch. I didn't want anyone to touch me, and I certainly didn't want to express my feelings physically toward anyone. I kept this up for two or three years, after which I discovered that I had a new body.

In some sense, the personality has not yet grown into the changing body. "It wasn't me; it was a whole list of things that were happening to me." Strange that a person should feel so powerless about the signs of emerging potency. Yet the teenager does recognize his power; he is at once player, field of play, critic, and cheerleader. What he needs is a coach he can trust during these months and years.

Lorna and Philip Sarrel use the word *unfolding* to describe the events of puberty, thereby naming it as a process, more comprehensive than biological change, but set in motion by the biological transitions, the hormonal storms that bring on puberty. Sexual unfolding has to do with learning whom you will become as an adult sexual being. It is active, with an agenda that, if hidden, is likely to cause problems. The developmental tasks that must be accepted during this time resemble the spiritual tasks of self-knowledge and self-acceptance. These tasks, formulated by the Sarrels out of their medical and psychological practice, can be listed in short order; their doing, however, continues for most of life.

1. First, the child needs to *adapt to the bodily changes of puberty.* This never occurs without ambivalence. For the girl it means, among other things, having breasts and knowing what it is to be stared at; for the boy it can be the feeling that, as his development is slower than girls his own age, he is never free from the tyranny of the athletic ideal. Even the most attractive and capable of boys can be terrorized by the categories of nerd and wimp. Adapting to the bodily changes of puberty is complete when the adult form of the body is accepted not only as "mine" but as myself, loved by me as I hope to be loved by others. Self-acceptance as sexual body is not made easier when one tries to say more than the truth. The media ideal of being "prettiest" or "strongest" makes self-acceptance a longer, slower process. Adolescence is the time for patience and common sense. Those who negotiate it most successfully recognize they have a good-enough body for what life expects of them. Serenity may be a strange virtue to propose for the stage of sexual unfolding, but it is the spiritual mark of self-acceptance crucial to this and later times of bodily change. Neither vanity nor perfectionism promote self-knowledge or self-love, for they judge, objectify, and attempt to improve the body as if it were a thing. The sense of adventure and curiosity to see what the future holds is the other side of serenity. It, too, is a spiritual state most attractive in people in transition, whether entering adulthood or preparing for death.

Recognizable signs of sexual arousal in girls and boys can be opportunities for their awakening to personal power, that is, the capacity for arousal that is known but need not be acted upon. When they understand what is happening when the unfamiliar feelings arise, they can learn to respond not with compulsion, but with options. Arousal is an occasion for articulating their potential as attractive and responsive partners. In its privacy, it calls attention to another source of power: they are awakening to moral agency. Parents and rule-makers provide guidance, but only the individual is responsible to choose when and with whom to express the new potential of the new body.

> I had a woman's body and the ability to do all kinds of things and have children. This was very exciting for me. However, in the back of my mind, I knew that I was playing with fire. I was well aware that I was still a girl in a body too big for me. Only now in my third year of college do I feel settled into my self and my body. My physical expressions of care have reached a happy medium between my uninhibited child and my closed-in adolescent. I think I still love my body and being a girl as much as I did when I was a child. Although the development of my person and sexuality have been ups and downs, I believe my experiences have put me in a place that is extremely comfortable for me and people around me.

Menarche (onset of menstrual flow in girls) and semenarche (the time of the first seminal emission in boys) are still probably the most important events that signal, in an externally intelligible way, the transformation of a child's body to that of a young adult. The circumstances around both these events are critical for developing good attitudes toward sexual experiences. One study showed that 90 percent of girls were using tampons two years after menarche. Such a simple thing as learning to insert a tampon, and being able to connect this with good feelings about vaginal penetration and containment is a step toward active ownership of their sexuality. Their feelings about crossing body boundaries and allowing something to enter interior space can color attitudes about having intercourse, in which a fairly large object is invited to penetrate her body space. The boy's experience with seminal emission, whether he is prepared for it or frightened by it, can have consequences for his attitudes and his performance as well. Kinsey's studies showed that its occurrence leads almost always to a fairly regular pattern of masturbation and wet dreams within just a few months. A much more recent study showed that while most parents discuss menstruation with their daughters and are aware when it has taken place, ninety-nine out of a hundred parents never discuss ejaculation or wet dreams with their sons. If they become associated with guilt and anxiety, he may program his own body to ejaculation by furtive and hurried activity followed by shame. Positive feelings about sex can be as simple and effective in origin as a sensitive and alert parent or relative able to talk to adolescents about these turning points calmly and with a tone of congratulations. These physical events are also psychosocial events, as is clear from studies of initiation and marriage customs. What has not been attended to is that they are also spiritual events. I believe that understanding of how our bodies prepare themselves for relationships of union ought to be a significant part of religious formation correlated to celebration of communion and confirmation, and carried through all the stages of adult education.

2. A second task has to do with *overcoming guilt, shame, fear, and childhood inhibitions about sex.* For some, especially those from dysfunctional or particularly rigid families, this is a process that takes people far into adulthood, and sometimes is responsible in its omission for the breakdown of marriages. A particular problem exists for girls and women in overcoming shame and inhibitions about sex. Boys, through their experience with self-pleasuring, may be able to overcome the negative childhood connotations of touching or "playing" with oneself. Religious and political gender-stereotyping has had a vested interest in keeping the myth alive that women, asexual until awakened by a man, are superior morally because more "innocent" about sex than men. But self-pleasuring, when free of compulsion, guilt, and conflict, can provide immediate experience of how sexual response feels, so that these become familiar. We learn what we like and what our body moves toward. We learn to integrate body and mind, fantasy and touch. We discover that it is possible at orgasm to lose control without dangerous consequences. All of this can help prepare a person for sharing sexual pleasure with another person. None of this is true, of course, when self-pleasuring is lost in guilt and conflict. When it makes people feel dirty, it should be avoided, for it is powerful symbolic action. What it means it will accomplish. Destructive as all addictions are, it is no less destructive when done because individuals feel they must do so in order to be normal and up to par. Anxiety makes for self-observation which interferes with good sexual response (and good prayer) as much as does guilt. The message communicated to youth should be neither fear of self-pleasuring nor pressure to do so, but simply that "about this we have no message from the Lord." Human wisdom is valuable; by it we learn from our mentors. But it should mandate or prohibit particular activities only if it serves the person's total development toward wholeness. To remain submerged in childish reactions and irrational fears is neither innocence nor virtue but pretense—ignorance pretending to superior morality. Childish inhibitions are inescapable since sexual expression belongs to the world of adults but we cannot make the successful transition into adulthood without overcoming them. Female inhibitions about owning sexual responses are as spiritually debilitating as male inhibitions about emotion or family inhibitions about the expression of intimacy. Where love is the vocation to which human beings are called, the skills of love in their appropriate context are occasions of grace.

3. *Shifting primary emotional attachment from parents to peers* seems to be the

only task of sexual unfolding that our society has set up institutions to support. The school system, the social and play networks without which children in small and two-career families could not survive, the communication industry including the television marketing to children, preteens, and teens and the world of Nintendo and computer games: all are organized toward the increasing independence from family of origin and the shift of allegiance from nuclear family to peers. The emotional attachment, of course, shifts in a healthy way only when those needs have been filled. Some commentators on the narcissism of the seventies and eighties have shown that the emotional neediness of an adult fixated on himself may in fact be the result of narcissistic needs not being sufficiently satisfied in babyhood. As a matter of fact, until these needs are met, that person is not likely to be able to enter into a spiritually satisfying relationship with another person. A kind of preevangelization period may be necessary in which the unconditional parent-to-infant kind of love is experienced as remedial. Strengthened by such assurance, one can feel "loved enough" to separate from the dependencies of childhood.

"In looking back on my life," wrote a thirty-six year old woman,

> I remember much of the time feeling like: 'Is that all there is?' I no longer view life in this way. My problem before was that I had so little respect for myself that no amount of love from others seemed to penetrate that. Now that I have grown up a little, this picture has changed. If I were to die today, I could honestly say that I have been loved enough, by God, by others and by myself.

One of the more subtle evidences of such emotional development is that the person is able to share the fact of her own sexuality with others who are significant to her. Fear that a parent or guardian will not accept one's relationship or even one's reality as a sexual person shows that perhaps one has not completed the emotional transition. Certainly this task is accomplished by trial and error, by taking risks and making mistakes, and slowly muddling through to maturity.

4. It is important that the young person taking control of his own sexual destiny *be able to communicate questions and feelings about sexual orientation*. This may sound strange to older adults who do not recall ever being asked about sexual orientation; moreover, only one is recognized as legitimate. But in our time, not only is there the increasing self-awareness of many gays and lesbians, but society is in fact being inched, reluctantly, toward the acceptance of difference. If a true pluralism rather than a polarization is valued, it becomes possible to name the strength and orientation of one's sexual desires. To be comfortable with them may be another matter.

FIGURE 1
THE KINSEY SEXUALITY SCALE

Exclusive hetero-sexuality	Predominant hetero-sexuality with incidental homo-sexuality	Predominant hetero-sexuality	Ambisexuality	Predominant homo-sexuality with more than incidental hetero-sexuality	Predominant homo-sexuality with incidental hetero-sexuality	Exclusive homo-sexuality
0	1	2	3	4	5	6

FIGURE 2
RELATIONSHIPS AND POTENTIAL EROTIC RESPONSE

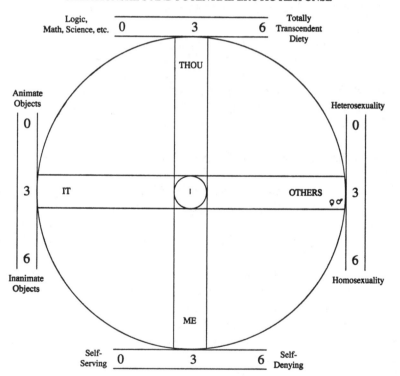

A number of cautions should attend the discussion of sexual orientation. No one should be pushed toward premature categorizing of oneself. The choice ought not be posed as between normal and abnormal; and in fact it is precisely not a choice. Those who have attained the maturity to tell their own stories report that it is experienced more as an awareness of what already is fixed. The choice is whether to accept it or not, whether to articulate one's sexual identity in terms of one's religious and social self-understanding or not, whether to acknowledge one's real feelings to family and friends. The way the identity issue is most often posed is: Am I homosexual, heterosexual, or perhaps bisexual? There is much to be said for avoiding such labeling until there is personal experience of genital relationship upon which to reflect. Sol Gordon is not just being silly when he says in public lectures that most of us are "trisexual. . . . We just haven't tried it yet!" There is seriousness in his assumption that one should not rush to categorize one's sexual identity according to what others imply about oneself, by extrapolating from one's fantasies or dreams, or even by generalizing from what occasionally stimulates arousal. One effect of the Kinsey scale (see Figure 1) was to show that human beings occupy a spectrum of possibilities, and are not necessarily grouped at either end of the polarization between exclusively homosexual or exclusively heterosexual. Moreover Kinsey noted that sexual orientation did shift in some people as they moved through life, through shades of homosexuality, bisexuality, and heterosexuality. [1]

A less well-known but more useful model for extending the range of what is perceived to be normal is that of William Stayton. [2] He begins with the assumption that human beings have potential for a greater range of erotic responses than is reflected in the Kinsey two-pole scale (from heterosexuality to homosexuality). Stayton's "panerotic" model (see Figure 2) supposes the individual to be capable of erotic responses to the Transcendent, the world of nature and animate objects, and the self. Rather than one scale, four scales are proposed for the identification of erotic potential. In addition to being locatable on a zero through six continuum in terms of attraction to same or opposite sex, the human being takes a position on a similar continuum from self-serving to self-denying activity, from erotic connection to the world of animate to inanimate objects, and on a scale from scientific rationality to total transcendence. The "erotic universe" within which one lives is, in this conceptualization, much richer than that of Kinsey. Stayton's model resembles a plus sign with the individual at the center and the four scales displayed at the four points of the compass. I find it a freeing vision for the individual, for through it the vocation of the human being as erotic subject can be construed in terms of development, not mere conformity. The whole universe, in Stayton's view, is a potential erotic turn-on. The potential for a sacramental view of the world of nature as well as of fellow human beings is increased when the whole of one's environment is viewed as capable of stimulating erotic and creative energy to be channeled into appropriate expressions. Moreover, such a possibility is affirmed by the experience of many whose erotic feelings are exercised on God or work or self-sacrifice or the wilderness. Interpersonal sexual expression does not account for the whole of human erotic energy. As there is a range of intelligence and aptitude, so there is a range in what is usually referred to as "sexual" arousal and fulfillment. This need not be judged as good or bad; it simply is. The characteristic of diversity is that most celebrated of God's creation, and "biodiversity" is the rallying cry of those who want to save the earth from destruction by a humanity that would sacrifice it in the name of economic development. The divine economy created and sustains the diversity of forms and the freedom that calls human beings to self-actualization. A monumental bias in favor of a social system that benefits from the procreative capacity of heterosexual relations and is threatened by nonprocreative sex is understandable; it is even understandable that it would put constraints on one form and not the other; but that the minority form would be denied existence, that persons who know themselves to be different in their most basic sexual orientation would be refused civil rights, persecuted and even killed by the more fanatic of the righteous majority—that is a sin against God the creator. The fact that an antigay rights position has been politicized by appealing to the fears and prejudices of people does not make it less but more of a spiritual issue in society. The politicizing of gender, race, and sexual orientation keeps one variation dominant for a time, but it does not change the fact that eventually the oppression of one group by the other is recognized and called what it is— sin—by at least some prophetic voices in society. The task of self-acceptance is made immeasurably more difficult for young people who feel "different," and believe they might be gay or lesbian. They cannot seek answers to their questions and fears as long as ridicule and persecution among their peers and condemnation by their elders threaten. Assistance in their search for self-knowledge, crucial to spiritual growth, is unavailable to them so long as they are prevented even from formulating the possibilities.

In the context of developing life, prior to the self-possession which makes one capable of freely giving oneself, the naming that comes with feeling the warmth and excitement of arousal, the erection or wetness of sexual readiness, is occasion not yet for sin, even in its classical definition, but for self-acceptance and self-articulation. When a person can admit to herself what she is feeling and know that it is normal for human beings, even though it may not be endorsed as the cultural norm, then she can thank God who in all the diverse works of creation is worthy of praise. What is required is not the precision of identifying oneself as a double zero or a 3.5 on the Kinsey scale; even less does one need to place herself somewhere on a scale of one to ten in terms of sexual self-knowledge, but it is always better to know than not know about ourselves. In so far as we are more ignorant than others about ourselves we do not own the bodies that we possess. Moreover, knowledge about ourselves can be neither obscene nor profane, for as sustained daily by the Creator, we are holy. It is absolutely essential for the integration of sexuality that we attain a positive self-image and a life in which our energies can be released productively.

5. Why should *"learning and communicating what we like and dislike"* be so difficult, when our consumer culture trains us early to make self-confident choices between goods, for no other reason than that we like one kind of cereal or athletic shoes better than another? To admit to liking anything regarding sex seems slightly immoral. I remember the peculiarly queasy feeling when, as a twenty-four year old, having said in ordinary gratitude to a man who brought a gift, "You know what I like," it was turned into a thing of shame when he repeated for another man present, "I know what she likes," giving it a particularly leering connotation. But to know what I like and dislike in terms of sexual (brain and skin, talk and touch) or genital (gentle or forceful) interaction is to be able to think of myself as appropriately autonomous and to be free enough, even with those I hope to please, that I can express preferences calmly and finally. As a matter of fact, surveys of students have shown that women and men consistently are wrong about what pleases the other. Women underestimated the percentage of men who like cunnilingus; men underestimated the percentage of women who enjoy fellatio. Since oral sex is more prevalent among unmarried young people than intercourse, it is particularly important that they have the language and the attitudes to be able to communicate openly about it. In old movies and new soap operas the most disconcerting scenes for women, in my view, are those in which she says, often repeatedly in words and body language, "No, I don't want to . . . don't" and yet does—most often by acquiescence, not force. The message here is that she doesn't know or can't admit what she really wants, and she always wants, but shouldn't—him. Such a conflicted sexuality is not adult or free or spiritually healthy. The women's movement, with its emphasis on women taking responsibility for their own sexuality, was necessary if only for this. Side issues like equal pay for equal work only make the essential issue—spiritual power over one's choices about how to act upon desire and arousal—more palatable to the arena of public discourse in a sexually immature culture.

6. *First intercourse* would not be the contemporary problem it has become if the previous five steps in the process of sexual unfolding were successfully negotiated. As marriage has been delayed and sexual double standards have come into disrepute, first intercourse has been to a great extent de-sacralized, almost a throwaway event, no more significant than later acts of coitus.

According to current research, half of American young women now have intercourse before they graduate from high school, compared to 23 percent in the 1950s. Those numbers may change with the greater approval of sex education in the schools that has come about through the need for AIDS education, but so long as intercourse with each other is the only method of experiential learning about sex, teenagers, with their overdeveloped sense of immortality and their underdeveloped sense of danger, are not likely to limit genital contact voluntarily. Fear of venereal disease has not been over-whelmingly successful as a motive for responsibility in sexual decision-making.

By the term first intercourse I describe not acts by which curiosity is satisfied, or a method of learning about sex which is not deterred by the anxiety of adults, but a ritual event in which two sexually maturing persons freely participate. Given the usual conditions of anxiety and limited preparation, the participants are likely to have very mixed emotions. One study showed that one-third of young women felt exploited by their first experience of intercourse, and while two-thirds reported feeling sexual pleasure, half of them also experienced high levels of guilt and anxiety. One-third of the total remembered no pleasure at all, but only guilt and anxiety. Of course, even as a sacred moment in sexual unfolding, the value of first intercourse has little to do with chronology, but rather with the spiritual meaning of a particular moment which provides a point of passage. When the partners are older, have worked up to it gradually as an appropriate symbol of their real relationship, have asked for and received each other's consent at crucial points, and are centered, loving, and tender, it is almost always an experience to be cherished. Thereafter every-thing—identity, social role, community status—will be different. "Honey-moon" stories, whether after or before marriage give concreteness to this spiritual meaning. From personal body world to the biosphere that surrounds the couple, everything has changed from the inside out.

> "I couldn't wait to see you," he said. "Are you all right?"
> "I hurt a little," she said.
> "But are you all right?" he said.
> "Never better!" she said.

The greatest discrepancies between male and female interpretations of first intercourse occur with the religious meaning assigned to "loss of virginity" for women. For men, early intercourse attempted or achieved is interpreted as the release of tension or the gaining of skill as a lover rather than the loss or gain of religious treasure. Some men, however, do speak about loss as one of the meanings of their first time. But it is different. It involves the loss incurred in moving into a new world, with a different emotional landscape from the old one. Sometimes it is seen afterwards to have been a mistake—perhaps destroying a friendship without the gain of a lover or wife. The dark side of the sacred is that it divides: what is not sacred is profane. There is no neutral ground. In religious literature about women, when the "loss of virginity" did not occur in a sacred context, that is, within the state of matrimony, the woman herself was seen as profaned by the material act, whether or not there was initiative or even active consent by her. The great majority of the students with whom I have discussed this material over the last twenty years indicated that first intercourse took place for them in situations with less than complete choice and with ambivalent feelings. But even "good-enough" sex can serve as pledge of what the future promises. The real first intercourse awaits as the person's moment of awakening to the possibilities of complete sexual union. The power of sexuality can be felt in the strength of the feelings that accompany intercourse—overwhelming exaltation or love or disappointment or disgust or contentment or sadness. Crying is not unusual for women or men, in the intensity of feeling evoked by the experience.

In my view the meaning of first intercourse as spiritual peak, moment of integration, final ending of inactive sexual existence, clear beginning of adult relational genital experience carries in itself, whether or not it is acknowledged, connotations of sacredness. Because it is a ritual moment, it participates in more than literal time. It is sacred passage, initiation into sacred sexuality of adult spiritual life, even if chronologically it is neither the first experience of coitus, nor coincides with physiological intactness of the hymen. Whatever the instances of penetration which preceded it, with or without orgasm, first intercourse, in the appropriate aesthetic and psychological context, can be the liturgy that heals and restores the person to spiritual centeredness, and so performs the deepest meaning of spiritual virginity: being a person who possesses herself, who is neither owned or taken away from her own vocation by someone else. It would not be unthinkable to establish this meaning in some communal and public fashion by celebrating solemnly the sexual relation by which one confirms spiritual relationship. This need is what precipitated the addition of matrimony as formal sacrament of the Christian church in the twelfth century. In fact, couples celebrating a second marriage know and practice this designation of a particularly solemn moment of togetherness as solemn first intercourse.

I do not believe religious thinkers should spend so much time deploring present conditions, when it serves no prophetic purpose. It is simply the fact that for the majority of young people their first coitus is not first intercourse; for young men rarely if ever was it so. Better to spend energy and wisdom learning what the empirical realities are, while giving people the meanings that enable them to extend the range of the sacred through their sexual lives. Those who speak for the Holy ought to diminish the power of the profane to falsely name sex; rather, in a strange reversal of role, they become the heralds of the profane.

Intercourse is the equivalent in sexual development of the stage of self-transcendence in spiritual formation. In a setting of mutual love and care, it is probably the most profound experience of self-transcendence. Union with something beyond and more than oneself is intimated if not temporarily achieved with first intercourse. Almost unthinkable for persons who have been happily sexually active is the willing return to a previously inactive existence. It is unfortunately also true that there is much pressure on young people in our society to have sex and demystify it. In a way, intercourse is still seen as a magic power. Some think that once they "do it" their fears and ambivalence will disappear. On the level of efficient causality, the only thing intercourse causes is pregnancy. On the level of symbolic causality, that which functions in personal development and interpersonal relationships, it causes what it means. For human beings, intercourse does not bring about love or clarity or tenderness that was not there before. It can be a sign of independence and assertiveness or dependence and submission, a glimpse of incredible loneliness or ecstatic union. It intensifies what is already there.

7. A seventh task of sexual unfolding is the *ability to cope with sexual dysfunction or compulsion.* While sexual dysfunction is not a universal experience, it is normal to experience some difficulties at various stages of life. Generally the word is associated with situations of failure or crisis in later life: too much stress, too much alcohol, too many medications, too little outlet for anger and other emotions. Few teenagers or young adults understand their sexual patterns well enough to have the courage to ask for assistance when there is a failure of social relationships or sexual fulfillment. Few parents or teachers are informed enough to intervene or even to recognize problematic patterns before they become antisocial or violent behaviors. Usually adults worry about the wrong things. Wanting to wear "sexy" clothes or read erotic material may be an entirely appropriate way of "trying on" a new identity as a being who is now permitted to be sexual. But there are problems in which intervention and help would be of great benefit, and would reduce greatly the amount of anxiety associated with sexual development. Most young men experience premature ejaculation. Many young women do not experience orgasm for some time after beginning sexual relations, even with a partner who is loved and trusted. There are degrees of difficulty and disturbance, from extreme shyness, which makes starting relationships exceedingly difficult, to the rarer paraphilias, by which an individual experiences arousal only in context of danger, violence, or fire or with the assistance of certain fetishes. Compulsive behavior can be recognized early. By compulsive behavior is meant sexual acting that is out of control,

repetitive, self-destructive, and usually not fulfilling.[3] Promiscuity of various forms fits this description, as does repetitive fixations or obsessions. Since multiple sexual experiences do not of themselves bring about psychological maturity, to dismiss compulsive behavior as something a person will grow out of when he falls in love is to deprive him of the healing that is available. It is no longer necessary, with all the professional services of counselors and therapists, for anyone to resign herself to a lifetime with a negative sexual image. Nor should the community be submitted to the possible harm consequent upon compulsive behavior. Obstacles to spiritual growth are meant to be removed, not accepted. For that we have the sacrament of reconciliation and the various liturgies of healing. The joy of adult living is practically constituted by the ability to love wisely and well. To help with that we have spiritual guides and mentors. Obstacles to sexual integration are meant to be removed as well, for they are obstacles to fulfilling one's vocation as a human being. Eventually persons will emerge who can minister to each other as sexual-spiritual guides, who can recognize problems and help persons grow from both points of view.

8. When coping mechanisms are in place for solving sexual problems, the next task is made much easier. The developing person needs to *come to understand the place and value of sex* in her life. All our human wisdom is achieved in the effort to find our way between excess and defect. One can never be too healthy, but health, though our concepts of it change, is a symbol for keeping all aspects of physical, psychological, and spiritual life in a "good enough" balance. More useful for life-guidance than concepts about the place and value of sex in life are practical models who have successfully been able to balance the many aspects of a full life. However rich the rules of thumb, norms and principles, role models, and community standards offered, the task remains that of the person whose sexuality is unfolding to find what is right for him. The turn to the inside, to the inner life, is characteristic of a moment of truth in spiritual and moral development. In this significant step, values are examined and reappropriated as one's own.

9. A ninth step toward sexual maturity is achieved in *becoming responsible about sex*. This represents the further development of an inner moral sense by which one makes decisions and governs one's actions. So long as a person depends upon external authorities for judgment about how to act sexually, she is vulnerable to compromise. The privacy, that is, the personal and intimate character of sexual situations, as well as the easily underestimated strength of the arousal, makes it unlikely that a person without an internal referent for his life will be able to respond to the human reality of a situation. A shift from external conventional morality to an internal morality of the heart is crucial to the developing sexual person. By definition spiritual awakening also requires the shift from the dualistic, outer-directed morality of childhood. In this step

as in others, the spiritual and the sexual stages may be negotiated simultaneously. Both sexual unfolding and spiritual awakening are produced and
enhanced by the personal appropriation of a responsible moral sense.

> Sex for young people is confusing. Parents leave signals that sex is
> bad, and television leaves you with the impression that sex is glamorous.
> Do you do what your parents want, or do you rebel against them to get
> attention? In my life, I seem to take the conservative road and do what I
> am "supposed to do." I am also a very disciplined person, and I wonder
> how many people fall victim to pressure by their friends. I sometimes
> wonder if I did too. After I did have sex for the first time, I still was not
> sure that my decision was right. When I told my friends about it they
> were disappointed in me. I am still confused about that, but now I must
> continue on with my decision to develop myself. Intercourse is not a bad
> thing, but knowing when you're really ready is the difficult part.

We know that those who feel comfortable with their own sexuality and
right about their behavior are more likely to plan for pregnancy or to avoid it.
They are also more likely to care about themselves and their partners by
practicing appropriate measures to see to it that disease is not spread by their
actions. Inauthentic action, bad faith, is not unusual if one or both partners
have failed to come to grips with the realities of their own sexuality. Because
the Catholic church teaches unambiguously that contraception is sinful, persons with an underdeveloped moral sense may go ahead with unprotected
intercourse, taking a chance, prudent thoughts overwhelmed by alcohol or
excitement. They remain childishly obedient at one level only to be immoral at
another, with added failures against the adult virtues of prudence and justice.
Persons who remain at childish stages of moral development fail to arrive at
responsible methods of decision-making appropriate to adult life, and are not
likely to progress in either their spiritual or sexual lives. They are more likely to
continue as the passive ground on which other forces are deployed: forces like
unconscious fears, unexamined traditions, and parental pressures. Sometimes,
for inexperienced people, lighthearted rules of thumb offer more help than
heavy-handed preaching. Such "rules" can give insight by surprising one into
attending to the radical value that could be missed in conventional rules. For
example: the question, "Should I have intercourse with my friend?" calls for the
following analysis. *Could you have initiated this step?* If the answer is no, if you
could not have initiated this sexual advance, you are not ready to acquiesce to
it. *Do you have options or do you feel that there is no other way to continue the
relationship?* If you do *not* have options, that is, to say not just yes or no, but to
renegotiate terms, for example, "Not tonight but ask me again a week from

tomorrow," then you are not free enough to give yourself now. *Do you need permission?* If you need permission, even mentally, from someone or can't wait to tell someone, you are not ready. *Could you give half your money to each other?* If you, as partners, could not share your bank accounts, you are not ready to share your inner mystery and sexual power. *Is this an ultimatum or other form of emotional blackmail?* If the urgency has taken the form of a demand or a dare, it is no longer an invitation to sexual participation, but violence, force, or trickery masquerading as lovemaking. Sexual self-sacrifice for another's good or at another's request is not love at all but idolatry. It has turned the other into God, and one's own genitality into the sacrificial offering.

10. Developing *intimacy*, that is, *combining love and sex*, is perhaps a greater hurdle than any of the above. It is almost countercultural since gender stereotypes have assigned sex to men and love to women. A male student wrote about the idea of sexual relations as a form of recreation, a "game to be played."

> The game consists of finding, seducing, and obtaining what could be described as a sexual conquest. The point of the game is to obtain sexual pleasure and this carries the connotation of victory. The male attitude has its foundation in the idea that sexual pleasure is an "it." The idea of getting "it" can be heard or seen in many environments. Often I have heard in the rest rooms of a night club statements like: "Are you going to get it tonight?" or "Is she going to give it up tonight?" An all-time classic was, "I'm glad I got a girlfriend at home because none of the girls here want it tonight." The general American male attitude not only deems sexual relations as a form of recreation but as a game to be won or an object to be conquered.

When sex is reduced to "it" and love to vague and romantic feelings that sweep one away, neither is worthy of an adult. The implication of this step in sexual unfolding is to see that, when love is present, an individual has the capacity and the versatility to make the gift of self in multiple ways. Intimacy connects what otherwise would be separated as the inner (love) and outer (sex). In the integration of inner and outer, when sex and love come together, a new dimension of being is experienced. This is the unitive glimpse; life is transformed when the spiritual and physical lives of partners can be shared. Those who have known such intimacy, whatever their problems, will always remain together because their union is spiritual. In the process of separation from childhood and from parents, the value of tenderness and touch is in danger of being forgotten. It will need to be recultivated in adult forms. Intimacy in fact produces and is the reward for adult vulnerability. All the ambivalence grown-ups feel about vulnerability, all their efforts at self-protection come into play when intimacy is involved. Social roles and personal histories tend to diminish rather than enhance the capacity for intimacy as people grow up. The four-year old who is not in the least abashed to ask to cuddle and who wants to touch always and everywhere learns quickly enough that there are complex rules. The easier way is to reduce the complexity by settling, as adults, for little or no intimacy. Less real listening, connecting, and communing are expected.

Intimacy for human beings, I propose, is the way to the experience of God as immanence, as Spirit. The spiritual issue that arises is that of respecting personal boundaries, while at the same time knowing that the temporary dissolution of boundaries is union. Human intimacy is so powerful and so difficult because it is real union yet always returns to the separateness of human bodiliness. We cannot know intimacy with God as immanent to us; we can only know intimacy, that combination of separateness and union, with other human beings. The family is for most people the primary school of intimacy and has much to do with determining a person's initial capacity for sharing of her life and herself. The window of opportunity, however, opens again especially wide at the time of life known as sexual unfolding. In the language of John of the Cross, sexual intimacy is the only effective analogy for expressing the meaning of intimacy with God. The insights that men acquire into the relationship between love and sex are needed by women; and women need to articulate for men what only they know from experience. When sex and love are connected in intimacy, sexual unfolding is complete.

The ten steps that have been discussed above are not stages which can be correlated to age or experience; they are rather steps or tasks in the first awakening phase of adult sexuality. Items on this common agenda continue to be the content for our personal inner work during the whole of life. In sexual-spiritual development the stages are not mutually exclusive, but overlap. The happy truth is that while this work is never done, neither is it ever too late to be begun.

STAGE TWO:
MAKING AND BREAKING COMMITMENTS

The second stage of adult sexual development is characterized by commitments. This raises a number of issues. Not only is there a range of commitments from which we choose how much to invest in a particular relationship, but there are also considerations beyond our control. The age considered appropriate for marriage and childbearing has varied considerably, with late-twentieth-century America showing a tendency toward later marriage and delaying the having of children. Economic status determines in part an individual's readiness for commitment as does membership in a group which is deemed eligible for public recognition of commitment.

There are few public liturgies celebrating stages of commitment other than marriage. "Living together" has become the way that a personal statement in the public arena about commitment can be made without asking for social support or religious blessing. The fact that such social statements about a couple's sexual commitment are now made and widely accepted signals the separation of sexual partnership from family, church, and legal structures. It focuses on a shift, particularly for a woman's sexuality, toward recognizing it as a matter of her human rights to manage, not the right of her father or of community officials. Such private arrangements are not universally celebrated, and for good reason. Unless partners, who wish to signify a degree of commitment to each other by living together without benefit of marriage have been able to communicate with their parents and networks of friends about the step they have taken, it can become a source of alienation and conflict. Some commitments then get in the way of others. Only the most spiritually mature can resist for a lifetime the temptation to resent the partner for the loss of closeness with parents and other friends alienated by their choices. Those who attempt to deceive relatives or employers on the assumption that they might condemn if they knew the truth have to bear the heavy burden of secrecy. Sometimes the combination of tension and guilt that is created destroys the very relationship which promised such complete sexual fulfillment. Every family has known what it is to battle over the conflicts that a sexual commitment provokes. When the conflict takes place openly, it forces people to take sides; when it is hidden, it produces conflict within oneself.

Spirituality by definition is connectedness. One of the spiritual issues of commitment has to do with community. It acknowledges that a sexual relationship is never solely a matter between consenting individuals. It involves all of the connections each of them brings to the relationship. It is strengthened or weakened by all the previous experiences each of them has had in trusting and trying out commitments. It affects, by its effects, the community in which they live.

Another issue is maturity. The saying of a total yes also depends on the ability to say no. Because many women have been conditioned to please, they can acquiesce without taking full responsibility for consent. A great step toward spiritual adulthood is taken with the ability to say the radical NO. That is why breaking off an unsatisfactory relationship, or rechanneling a less than fulfilling one, can be required by one's own integrity. It is a matter of justice that a partner is not deceived when the level of commitment is not mutual. As much as reaching out to others is a law of spiritual growth, co-defining of boundaries is essential to honest commitment. These are skills without which adult character development cannot proceed. All commitments need not be permanent; some are more growth-producing because temporary. There is pain when a relationship that hoped for permanence ends, but even that ending can serve growth with more self-knowledge and a fuller investment in one's next commitment. But it is precisely in the face of painful necessity—accepting what is beyond one's power to change—that persons enter their spiritual depths.

Making commitments does not always mean the investing of sexual energy in genital relationships. It is also appropriate to make one's commitments to social issues, to professional or leadership positions, before or in place of choosing a partner to share one's life. It is possible that the commitment of one's time, talent, energy to the vocation within the community that one has discerned calls for the temporary or permanent cessation of particular sexual possibilities. This is part of the mystery of the individual call and response. It is hard for people of our time to understand why it was necessary for so many centuries for women to be harnessed to the task of reproduction in such a way that they had no alternatives. All other commitments, it was decided for them, were subordinate to the commitment to motherhood. That attitude, though discredited, has not entirely disappeared.

The experience with commitments, how they grow and die and sometimes are sustained for life, is to me the greatest evidence of what it means to say that human beings are made in the image of God. Like God we wait upon the freedom of others, rejoicing with their yes to us, bearing no resentment with their no. Human fidelity is a gift given not once for all but minute by minute. It is unlike God's fidelity in that human beings are subject to time and change; God's fidelity implies eternity. Human beings court and woo each other, promising fidelity even as the Scriptures show God calling for love and commitment. The whole of Psalm 78 is a summary of God's call to the people and their conflicted awareness of disappointment and hope. The psalmist cries out, "I commune with my heart in the night; I meditate and search my spirit; 'Will the Lord spurn for ever, and never again be favorable? Has his steadfast love for ever ceased? Are his promises at an end for all time?'" (Ps. 77:6–8) We wait with open heart for hoped for favors. Zephaniah says to Zion: "The Lord your God is in your midst, a warrior who gives victory; he will rejoice over you with gladness, he will renew you in his love; he will exult over you with loud singing as on a day of festival" (3:17). The image of courting, exacting, and making promises suggests a kind of sexual humility. We know from bitter experience that forced or tricked acquiesence is utterly without value.

At the second stage of sexual spiritual development, commitment is the challenge. But "Be mine" and "I am yours" also have a dark side. From the man who truly believes that he has a right to exact sexual favors for buying dinner for a woman to the one who murders the estranged spouse who has obtained a court order against him, the newspapers are full of evidence of confusion between commitment accepted on trust and ownership of another as property. Not even marital commitment solemnly declared before God and the human community gives anyone else the right to a person's soul. Development in the spiritual lives of persons in sexual partnerships must assure that not only are they able to make full-hearted commitments that they intend for life, but that also they are able to accept with equanimity when commitments made to them are broken. This is not weakness. A person with a poor self-image cannot accept it. This is hope, the relaxed recognition that only God ultimately is God. Sexual partnership can only mediate the Spirit if it does not try to usurp the part of the Spirit.

STAGE THREE: COMMITMENT IN MARRIAGE

The public call to genital intimacy in marriage is a call to deeper communion. That the genital union is accomplished also as a joining of incomes and households between two particular persons, each with different biological, cultural, and psychological heritage is an investment toward improvement by diversity. In this encounter, if it is to be authentic, each partner accommodates the other, but in such a way that each remains faithful to self. The partners do not fuse; they do not abandon their separate selves. Authentic sexual love involves both identification with the other (giving) and opposition to the other (keeping, taking). Each participates in the other in a kind of "dance" reminiscent of the image of *perichoresis* used in trinitarian theology. They are to be respectfully attuned both to self and partner, desiring both to express their own pleasure and to be pleasing. The novelists use phrases like "lost in each other" which reflect something of the special moment in which both know there is no way out except through the completion of the self-giving. The boundaries are not lost; they are allowed to be crossed, so that the impossible thing, the gratuitous act of finding someone who cares, is accomplished. That is of course also the source of the loneliness, the sense of betrayal and the shame when and if it is found, at the other side, to be not so.

But it does not always end there. The caricature of the stages of marriage as consisting of three stages, "kiss, bliss, and hiss," is true precisely as a caricature. The call to communion that is heard in intimacy and accomplished in genital union is not fulfilled in that union, but it is satisfied. It is meant to be experienced more than once: satisfaction increases appetite. The dynamic of genital sex is a hunger that cannot be permanently satiated, but in its periodic satisfying we become more fully ourselves, more not less aware of boundaries and limits, more capable of loving not divinely but humanly. It is made not to challenge the divine economy, but to sustain one in the routines of domestic life. The very rhythm of sex may contribute to its bad reputation among religious thinkers, who have been known to overvalue permanence. As James Nelson shows in his reflection on male sexuality and masculine spirituality, there is a dichotomy illustrated by the symbols of phallus (the erect male organ) and penis (the inert, flaccid organ). He claims that the overvalue of phallus with its representations of strength, dominance, and determination lead to a rejection of penis and its associations with vulnerability, mortality, smallness, and softness. The dichotomy between these two images produces a separation of the qualities associated with each, and an eventual hierarchy in which the "mighty erection" comes to characterize the psychological state of the normative male. This rejection of penis, Nelson claims, is a rejection of an integral part of the human, an alienation of part of the self. He emphasizes that in its soft and flaccid form, the penis is a perfectly good image of maleness, yet one that, with all its associations, remains unintegrated into male spirituality. When men reject these qualities of penis, Nelson claims, they project them upon women. Women are "seen to be small, soft and vulnerable, qualities inferior to the phallic standard" which men associate with "true masculinity."[4] The Holy Spirit's message, that can be heard through the ebb and flow of the genital encounter, is that when physical urgency is allowed to become part of the whole of life, not split off, not expected to carry the whole of love, not used or feared, the authenticity of the process of risk, openness and surrender can emerge. The genital call is not to genitality but to humanness, to affectivity and tender care of oneself and another because that is how the creator God intimately loves the universe.

We are moved by intercourse (and not only in its ideal or perfect form) toward maturity. Much of that movement is toward the acceptance of finitude—that is, away from obsession with the genital. Genital fixation promises to meet every unmet need, and then always breaks that promise. Not the least of the personal and social benefits of marriage is that it moves people toward more generalized sexual awareness. The promise of sacramental marriage, that sex can mediate the holy for good faith partners if they allow it, is not delivered automatically by intercourse; the holy is discovered in the search to be a full human being. Whether a couple's lovemaking will be integrated with those depths or split off from them is the challenge of authenticity. It gets asked in new ways many times in the course of the sexual passages of a normal life.

The rhythm of involvement and detachment into which marriages settle is the condition for the growth of sexual life. The detachment is not denial or avoidance; it is rather the natural outcome of a pattern of desire and satisfaction, striving and rest. The pleasure is served by the separations as much as by the coming together. Capacity for enjoyment is the underlying dynamic. The optimum rhythm for intensity is discovered by the couple as they track their individual pattern. It would be disrupted by a desperate search for continuous gratification. This inevitably causes unhappiness. As it becomes a consuming need for more uninterrupted pleasure, or love, or service, it is revealed for what it is—the will-to-dominate in the guise of neediness. The partner cannot enter into such a relationship without losing authenticity. Who can never get enough, can never really grasp the freedom or enjoyment of love. Whoever tries to avoid all the pain that comes from separation or absence loses what he most desires because there is no reverence. The sexual endowments of the partner have become objects, which can never surprise him. The needy and dependent attitude vitiates a genital relationship in other ways as well. The partner, to maintain her integrity, her freedom to choose, and her very identity, has to withdraw or be partner to an illusion that has no future as a relationship. Inevitably it will disappoint and be replaced by another illusion. Following the ultimate mystery of life and death, accepting the weakness and limitation of love is key to its strength.

One of the problems of women in marriage is that they expect too much, as if the state of matrimony were in itself capable of delivering fulfillment. Women's culture, as girls are conditioned to it, sets them up to expect that a man should be able to make them happy. He is expected to conform to the illusion or his very success as a man in their eyes is threatened. From the outside it appears to be so in other marriages. But happiness can't be handed over from one person to another; nor ought it to be the goal of life. Happiness is better seen as the by-product, the halo-effect of a life well lived, a blessing which rides piggy-back on things less glamorous: food and shelter and work worth doing, with a balance of nurturing and challenge. Men, the researchers report, don't really expect happiness in marriage, so while they are not so easily disappointed, they are not that much better off. The challenge is to sustain intimacy in a familiar relationship. It is equally the challenge of prayer. Like any long-standing relationship when it grows stale, only new depth can revive it.

For Christians the potential sacramentality of marriage is formally witnessed and invoked by the community celebration. While the wedding is not the marriage and therefore not the sacrament, it is the public moment when the meaning of what in fact is taking place is affirmed to be a saving act of God. Without in any way diminishing their freedom, the married couple, by accepting a life of sexual commitment and sharing, is declared an event of salvation for the world. It may have been so before, but it is now known to be such by and in the church community. This means an extraordinary thing: that sexual partnership can carry out God's saving activity in the world, and not just mystically, secretly, or privately, but publicly and officially as the action of the institutional church. It is the Spirit which makes, not now new things, but old things new. Here we don't choose between sex and love. They are reciprocal. Sexuality has become in this couple an embodiment of the great Mystery of Reconciliation (Eph. 5). Here is begun a relationship that can carry out in history not just the mysteries of creation and redemption, but especially of sanctification. Marriage is the sacrament, with the eucharist, closest to the Holy Spirit as God's immanence teaching us about Christ, by teaching us what it means to be human.

But how are spouses taken up into this mystery?[5] According to Karl Rahner, it is not the efficacy of their love, nor their baptism. It is their implicit intention to do what Christ and the church do, that is to identify their conjugal love with Christ's paschal attitude. The theologians of marriage have tried to put words to what this attitude is: permanence, fidelity, fruitfulness. The minimal condition necessary for making the marital consent a true human act in the domain of sacrament is to intend what the Spirit intends. Where there is no trace of faith, of course, nor any desire for grace or salvation, there would be doubt that a truly sacramental intention would be present. But then there is no spirituality and it is doubtful that an intimate relationship could take hold and endure.

Some will object to such a nonrestrictive approach to the capacity of sexual partnership to achieve sacramental status. But even classical Catholic theology of marriage insisted that the public ceremony does not add, but only witnesses to what is realized in the consent and conjugal relations of the couple. The authorization is not so much directed to the couple, as it is to the congregation present that this couple is to be recognized and supported as an authoritative center of God's loving action. There are degrees of sacramental status. An analogy from ministry may be helpful. I would argue that as nonordained ministry is to the order of ministry, so sexual love is to the sacrament of marriage. The kind of action that is deputized by ordination is possibly already and also present in the nonordained; the kind of action that is authorized by a church wedding is possibly already and also present in those whose conjugal relations are not ordained as formally, visibly sacrament.

There is no order other than the sacramental order, and that is a dynamic and developing process, not a conversion from profane gestures and attitudes to holy ones. The priest or minister who presides does not strip sex of its concupiscence. God lives and acts in all human beings, moving them to their love when and if they are so moved. The Catholic claim is that Christ took up marriage's meaning and its power to help in his work in the world. An essential part of the meaning and power of marriage is sexuality. If, for Christians, marriage cannot be a natural contract, neither can sex be profane. The sacraments are not in some secret locked religious sector. They are the manifestations of the Spirit in the world.

STAGE FOUR: PREGNANCY AND PARENTING

> True liberation of myself as a woman means, for me, the ability to delight in my body. It means my ability to accept the pleasures associated with my body, to control the functions of my body until the internal and external structures accept the pregnancy. In this sense childbirth can be an experience that I can look forward to as a pleasurable body experience.

The spiritual significance of pregnancy and parenting, one would think, would have been highly developed by women reflecting and writing about these key experiences. But it is not so. Perhaps one should not be too surprised. In the past, the process of reproduction, particularly women's part in it, was so associated with nature, the world of animal instinct, and the pain that was so presumed to be punishment for sin that it hardly qualified as spiritual. At present, the concern of women in process of liberating themselves from immersion in the body has led them to neglect, if not reject, the praising of bodily processes that are peculiarly female as places of access to religious experience. They want to get out of the body, to get into the intellect; to identify not with the family but with the public forum. In some ways women in a feminist and postfeminist age are on a journey of transcendence, which is not conducive to extended consideration of the joys of motherhood.

But the potential is there. Pregnancy and childbirth are experiences as closely related to the creativity of God as any of the experiences of "generation" available to a man. He is distant from the process, participating in it only by knowledge, not feeling. He has no direct experience of conception (nor does she) and is only able to track his part as causal by interpretation; socially, legally, religiously, the child is defined as his. But after having apparently accepted that birth belonged to the world of women, fathers are now finding ways to participate physically and psychologically in the spiritual event of birth.

A mother, by necessity, is wholly involved. The creative power of life changes her body visibly. But if her network of support is not deep and loving, the pregnancy may be experienced more as a burden than a rapture. Moreover, the religious valorization of motherhood in Mary, the mother of Jesus, was often so rapturously articulated that it left the ordinary woman's experience of motherhood far behind in the shadows. These may be some of the reasons that a spirituality of pregnancy and parenting, relating directly to the sexual facts, rather than to the sentimental memories of others, is still undeveloped. It is almost remarkable that birth was so long accepted as belonging to women, and women as belonging to nature. In the image of openness, birth is marked as belonging to the world of Spirit. The openness of childbirth is more dramatic than the openness of breathing in and out, but it is the same motion. The image most common for the Spirit is that of breath. As Washbourne describes it, childbirth also recalls the openness of digestion and orgasm. All this "taking in and giving out" may be physical in its motions, but it is spiritual in its meaning. As Ruysbroeck wrote, "The love of God is an indrawing and outpouring tide."[6]

In Washbourne's words, "It is also a cosmic event—a glimpse into the nature of life itself, into my own birth and into my own death. . . . This is ecstasy. To surrender oneself, to participate in and to feel the force of creative action. It is the spirit. In the femaleness of my own body I have experienced creation groaning, the spirit moving. I know it and am thankful for it."[7]

Understandably, most women have commented on the spiritual experience of pregnancy more in relation to the love they have with their husbands than any sense of identification with God in creativity. In the film *For Keeps,* the young mother, responding to the wonder of her husband when he felt the fetus move for the first time, said to him, "It's you, it's you inside me." The unity of the act of intercourse with the pregnancy and delivery is inescapable. Similarities between the physiological changes in a woman that lead up to orgasm and those that lead to birth have been noted. Giving birth is a sexual event in the sense that it is the culmination of an act of intercourse, another moment of surrender to natural body rhythms and processes, submitting before the mystery of life.

There are issues about practical life that are raised by the decision of a couple to have children.[8] Their sexual life changes, often for the worse, since aspects of pregnancy and parenthood can conflict with eroticism: there is less time to cultivate their relationship; she may feel less attractive; they may be anxious about the increased commitment required of them; he may have to deal with unacknowledged resentment over loss of her exclusive attention. Most new parents show a decline in intercourse frequency throughout the first year after the birth of the baby. Moreover, there are conflicts inherent in the very newness of the situation. It is impossible, no matter how much reading or consulting of others one does, to be completely prepared for what will happen when a completely needy person enters the system that had found its own equilibrium. Many women are aware that breast-feeding their infant can arouse distinctly erotic sensations. Some who have not understood that this is a normal physiological response have been very upset by these feelings. Actually, besides being pleasurable, they may aid in the formation of a close and loving bond between mother and child. The sexual life of new parents is characterized by continuing readjustment. Creativity, change, and potential growth are the other side of the new problems.

Being parents means dealing not only with the adjustments necessary in the couple's own sexual relation but also with the facts about children's sexuality, providing sex education and dealing with the issues that arise on a day-to-day basis. Touching and expressing love in a warm and physical way is basic, as is answering any and all questions from earliest childhood in a way that is as candid and relaxed as possible. That may mean, as at any stage, saying, I don't know but will find out. Feeling good about our bodies, including the way we look and smell and feel, even when ill or untidy, is an aspect of self-worth that can be taught. Negative messages about the genitals are communicated without words unless parents are very aware of body language. Moreover, street language or clinical accuracy with regard to sexual terminology is not enough. Most children are able to use the term penis easily. They are not so well informed about the female equivalent. The vulva, which includes the outside part with the clitoris and labia as well as the inner part, the vagina, is the appropriate term for the female genital structure. The difference such naming makes should be obvious: to emphasize the vagina, or worse, refer to it as a hole, is to suggest that the only thing the female contributes is a place for the penis to enter; to emphasize the whole of the vulval area makes the point from the beginning to boys as well as girls that female sexuality is neither derived from nor less significant than male sexuality. Parents need also to provide access to a truly usable erotic or poetic language without which some dimensions of sexual experience can't be understood or expressed.

Between the ages of one and two, children discover and appear to intentionally pursue self-stimulation for the pleasure it brings them. After the age of two it usually becomes a more private and solitary experience as they learn more about social expectations. Genital self-touching by children is not harmful or wrong and should never be punished or shamed. As in everything else regarding etiquette, they need to be carefully guided toward the distinction between public and private behavior. While sex education is accepted by most parents as their right and responsibility, it is never accomplished in a one-time talk. Yet, as an explanation of the process of reproduction, it takes place most often, when it does at all, as a one-time ordeal. Less than 15 percent of parents discuss reproduction with their three to eleven-year-old children according to the research of Lorna and Philip Sarrel; for those who do, it is a one-time event and often described in terms of animal or plant life. Teaching college students, a significant number of whom are over twenty-five years of age and have been married and given birth, I have been impressed with how many are learning for the first time basic biological and physiological facts about their own and their partner's sexual functioning. How can they reassure their nine to fifteen-year-old sons and daughters about what is to be expected? More importantly, how can they communicate to them that their feelings, fantasies, crushes, and curiosities are normal and healthy? How can they, especially, help them to learn that even though they may have done some things they are ashamed of, they and their sexual urges are not shameful? Of course parents ought to be so comfortable with all the aspects of sexual behavior that they can be explicit with their children about what they approve of and what, on religious or other grounds, they do not. Children overwhelmingly accept their parents' values; greater problems ensue when they do not know them or assume their parents to be more "strict" than they are. Studies have shown that parents and children are far off the mark when they are asked to describe what attitudes the others have regarding sex. Generally the children rate their parents more conservative than they describe themselves, and the parents think of their children as more liberal. One study found the identical phenomenon between teachers and parents in a school which was considering implementing a sex education curriculum. The teachers predicted that the parents would object to certain topics. When polled directly, they in fact agreed that those topics should be included in the curriculum. Communicating about our values is not only good for those who love and wish to guide; it is also essential to our own spiritual development to learn to articulate values so that they can be examined. The turn to the inner life for guidance is a turn to the Spirit and may well be motivated by the desire to say to the children what the adults themselves believe. Fear of putting what is valued into words does not preserve it as a stronger value; rather it keeps adults' and children's inner and outer lives at a distance, and often in contradiction. That is something that makes clear choices even harder. Some might think that if there were less talk about sex, there would be less experimentation. That is certainly true with regard to the kind of talk about sex that "sells" it: the rock video and soap opera, the commercial with its subliminal messages. The shock value that is released when an entertainer like Madonna connects the externals of sex with the externals of religion keeps both on the consumer side of culture. The kind of talk that integrates sex-talk into the love life of the family—religious, ethical, relational—takes away the lure of the forbidden and the opportunity to use it to rebel against parents, family, and religion at times of anger or need for separation.

"Procreation is not the primary purpose of sexuality," wrote one of my students, "but the development of mature spirituality could be the ultimate purpose of procreation." She went on to speak about how her own children's emerging sexuality challenged her to change her own attitudes. Love is the energy that makes rethinking possible.

"If the day comes when I can love everyone I meet in the way that I love my own children, and really know that they are my children, I will have reached the ultimate goal of all spiritual searching," she concluded.

Deciding not to have children[9] also has implications for spiritual growth and sexual life. There may be the special bond where the commitment is unambiguously for the sake of each other and not for children. Enhanced sexual satisfaction along with additional time to commit the energies released by the love relationship to the world's problems may be sought. Along with the pluses of a child-free sexual partnership come minuses—a different kind of intimacy and playfulness that is lost, a sense of time and history that is marked by the children's stages of growth. No heirs. The spiritual challenge of parenting or being generative without parenting in the fourth stage of adult sexual development is that of grief and change. When we learn to grieve a particular loss and to come through again, the passion and resurrection are taking deeper hold in our lives. The mystery of life through many little deaths forms the heart of sacramental transformation. It is the way that we live out at this stage our link to the great spiritual story.

STAGE 5: LOVING AGAIN AFTER LOSS

Paradoxically, the fundamental experience of sexed beings is separateness, singleness. But that is different from the threat of permanent separation. Love was defined by Paul Tillich as the reunion of the separated. The process of reunion includes and transcends loss and loneliness. It would not be better for a person to avoid the experience of genital encounter just to avoid the experience of loss. As the natural unfolding of a human process it is a place of God's action and a work of grace. Said in another way, any relationship which is honestly entered upon and followed through, but which ends, can prepare one for the next relationship. The hope and the experience of some is that love after a loss can catch up all that was good in the earlier one while striving for that which it lacked. It can also provide a school of tolerance for imperfection. After a great loss it is not unusual for individuals to attempt to protect themselves by withdrawing into isolation. But loneliness itself can become part of the remedy. Through another experience of sexual love, they can allow themselves to be known and loved with fewer demands and expectations, with their known flaws and limits. The vulnerability of a genital relationship helps people to see and show themselves without pretended strength or beauty or virtue. And sometimes honest, self-conscious introspection can lead to contemplation, that is, one could pass from a consciousness of oneself as imperfect to a willingness to be oneself. Even the lost or failed relationship reflects the longing that seeks communion with God.

The issues involved in the stage of sexual life that are here named in terms of the recovery of love are difficult ones. This stage may be brought on by disenchantment with sex life, by growing out of gender roles as defined within a relationship, by the extraordinary demands of dual careers, by competition and envy between partners, by a new infatuation and genital infidelity, by tragic and violent experiences of loss, such as rape or some other trauma. An abortion could bring on this crisis. So could the death of a spouse, an experience of betrayal, or even a poorly understood mid-life crisis.

Those in helping professions and ministries of healing have developed some clear-cut guidelines to help persons survive these crises.

1. They need to make sense of their previous situation—learn from it and deal with the anger and hurt that remains. Anger causes more spiritual problems if it is not expressed appropriately. In a situation of divorce, it is the function of the courts and the vocation of lawyers to enable the client to express feelings in ways that are objective yet personally healing. The process for annulment intends the same effect. Techniques taught by those in various ministries include journaling (to find and understand patterns in one's own behavior), support groups, mentors, networks of friends, new nonsexual involvements and causes (which help recover self-esteem).

2. Persons who have been hurt need to adjust expectations and dreams and reset goals: What do you want sexually? Tenderness? adventure? assertiveness? independence? What do you want spiritually? Healing? forgiveness? the sense of life as a call to something greater? serenity? Sometimes a dimly perceived need to improve oneself, a desire to be what one recognizes in another, is at the source of what is mistaken for sexual attraction. One has to be able to ask whether the desire is spiritual, whether it points to oneself rather than another as what is necessary for enhancement of life. Maybe she doesn't need or even want the man with whom she is infatuated, but needs to develop in herself the qualities that are so irresistible in him. This may be an occasion for a person to set, for the first time in her life, a spiritual goal.

3. Persons who have been hurt need to be flexible and open to the new. The chance to begin again, painful as it may seem, is a gift. Rebirth is a spiritual reality. The dynamic here, as throughout the stages of growth, is not toward "spiritualization" but toward integration into the whole of life. The restoration of balance produces immeasurably more sexual and spiritual energy. When the drain of continually having aspects of oneself battle each other is slowed, life can become more full.

The harshness of life, the losses that have been sustained, make it necessary for a person to achieve a new acceptance of life as it really is, its imperfection, its failure to deliver on its promises. Sometimes the contemplation of such things leads to insight: perhaps there was no promise broken by life at all; perhaps it was only the person's own assumption that he could avoid the common problems of life, and be treated as a special case. The loss of a sexual hope or relationship is to be taken seriously and pondered in faith. It provides entry to the paschal mystery in our bodies and spirits. This mystery of death as condition for transformed life is only accepted when all the frantic searching for the way it used to be is let go, and the meaning of relationships become as much faith and hope, courage, temperance, and wisdom as they are love.

Disillusionment helps her let go, drop the overseriousness, laugh at her slow liberations from the needs . . . to serve . . . or to be the best . . . or to never suffer. No longer does she need to say hers is the best love story in history, the only marriage that never failed, the sex that made the earth move. Now he can be more relaxed—a mentor to all other lovers who are imperfect and yet have a right to survive. It is spiritual growth that is authentic because it no longer needs to prove anything, but its very existence is witness to the victory of the Spirit. In the novel *The Unbearable Lightness of Being*, the character Tomas expresses this insight.

> "Haven't you noticed I've been happy here, Tereza?" Tomas said.
> "Surgery was your mission," she said.
> "Missions are stupid, Tereza. I have no mission. No one has. And it's a terrific relief to realize you're free, free of all missions."[10]

STAGE 6: KEEPING ALIVE WHILE AGING

At mid-life, it is time for a review and another chance at the developmental tasks that are part of the process toward a problem-free sexual life. These can be formulated in many different ways. For our purpose here, let us combine them into four recurrent tasks. The first is learning about and accepting our sexual selves. At the time of middle age, what has been called the "age of grief," this is a different task from adapting to the sexual bodies of youth; it is to learn to expect and enjoy sexual vitality in a body that must be accepted as aging. We also need to continue to manage sexual experience without fear, victimization, or destructiveness to ourselves or others. Finally, we need to understand and accept our intense feelings and keep sexual pleasure alive throughout our lives.

Obstacles to sexual growth at this stage include an intentional or unintentional inhibition of the sensual self. Sometimes people feel that they should no longer allow their bodies to be legitimate sources of sexual pleasure, for whatever reason, from the death of a spouse to a change in the familiar patterns of arousal. Some develop difficulty in trusting a partner because of things that have happened in the history, sexual and otherwise, of their relationship. Struggles with sexual identity may occur and loss of sexual appetite may produce confusion and perhaps loss of self-esteem. Lovemaking can become an adventure again with the same partner if new ways of mediating excitement and anticipating pleasure are found. I think that taking a positive attitude toward sexual life is the primary challenge of this stage, rapidly becoming the most extensive one, really a stage of stages. The ambivalences of youth, along with the need to conform of early adulthood can now be exchanged for a serene appreciation and comfort in the body. God wants, said Catherine of Siena, not success but great desire. Does the hope for orgasm figure here at all? About the less frequent experience of intercourse that accompanied their older years one woman said, "It's not the penetration that's so great; it's the feeling of being overwhelmed by something much greater than you . . . and it comes not from the outside but from the inside." One comment that might be made on this reflection is how much it resembles the classic description of the spiritual experience; another is the deprivation that is undergone when it is no longer an expected part of life.

With the end of fertility for whatever reason comes another opportunity for sexual and spiritual growth. Hysterectomy or prostate surgery, though they are thought not to affect potential for orgasm, will inevitably change the sexual expression of the relationship. It will not end it unless the partners see it as ended, but even the time of abstinence necessary for healing will likely affect the frequency of intercourse. There are, of course, many ways of making love. The end of fertility need not be the end of sexual satisfaction. The loss of a partner can mark for many the end of genital experience and the particular kind of sexual fulfillment that their marriage offered, but even that is not the end of a person's sexual life. Sometimes the rediscovery of self-pleasuring can provide an arena in which a person can rework a personal failure into a triumph by changing its outcome through fantasy. Self-pleasuring can coincide with self-forgiveness to create a new confidence and the expectation of future love. The key to self-esteem, one would have learned who negotiated all the stages prior to this, is to be able to experience mistakes and failures as lessons, and then to try another way. Choosing abstinence can also be a wise sexual choice in middle age as in adolescence, with equally acceptable sexual alternatives. As one student wrote, "Through my soul searching, I know that, although I am a sexual person, for right now, genital sex is not for me. And I'm not sure really why that is. Is it because sex has been a battle ground for most of these years of my life?" Abstinence from intercourse is not the same as relinquishing one's sexual vitality. The rediscovery of "sex without sex" is an unanticipated result of widespread fear of contracting the AIDS virus. People abound, of course, who died sexually at forty—and weren't buried until eighty. In my view that is tragic, a loss in the spiritual as well as the physical realm. To accept the loss of one's sexual life is as unnecessary and preventable as to give up one's intellectual life without regret.

Research on the effects of menopause is attempting to separate the myths and uncritical associations from the empirically established effects. Even those which are found to be causally connected to menopause do not occur in every woman. Menopause can produce a sense of fragility or vulnerability in some women and lead even to agoraphobia. Indirectly this all affects sexuality. Touching makes them more anxious, not just about sexual advances but even children or grandchildren coming into their body space. Some have generally negative feelings about being touched. Hormone replacement can make a difference. Changes in vaginal lubrication lead to dryness and hence to pain and thus to avoidance. In line with wholistic theories about mind-body interaction it is known that continued sexual stimulation and vaginal penetration prevent some of these changes. Those who go for long periods of time without sex are most seriously affected by vaginal changes. Women themselves report decreased sensitivity of the clitoris. For those women for whom it was the primary source of sexual stimulation, its loss of sensitivity is particularly disturbing. The global character of the fear was expressed by one woman in the question: "How do I know I am alive if I do not feel as intensely as I did?" Sexual desire does not appear to be affected directly by lack of estrogen, but it is diminished by the reduction of testosterone (produced by the ovaries) which influences sexual desire in both sexes. There is research into testosterone therapy, but medical doctors are often unwilling to consider this: "after all," one said, "we don't want our women going around with beards and big muscles." The ovaries produce estrogens, progesterone, and testosterone; yet even when there is no immediate medical problem with them, they are routinely removed in the hysterectomy on the premise that they are vulnerable to cancer and it is better to take it all out at once, than to have to operate again later. Better for whom? The crisis of menopause, not less when it comes prematurely by surgical intervention, can be a journey which moves one from the head to the deepest regions of the personality.

Experience of illness or any loss of bodily power is difficult because we lose control, and seem, at times to be on the verge of disintegration, yet through this experience of darkness we come to see more clearly, to love more creatively, and become more truly human. The path through darkness is in fact the way of integration. The age of grief marks women, not only in its arriving—with their experiences of inner, not just vicarious or outer loss, but in their having to live with it for thirty or forty years.

If people believe that sex is the vehicle of love and intimacy but see it in an overly instrumental way, they are left with the feeling of a loss in their ability to love as the vehicle slows down. Men at this stage begin to question their manhood, and perhaps seek a younger partner to excite through novelty what has lost its urgency through familiarity. Usually around age forty-five or so a mid-life crisis for men occurs. Besides the affair or divorce, a period of impotence is not unusual; at the time of the wife's menopause, a sexual dysfunction or withdrawal is occasionally reported. After age sixty, more serious problems may develop because of his psychological reaction to his physiological changes. Envy of the partner can also cause problems, especially if she begins to thrive just as he appears to be going into decline. For her, simultaneously, success and vitality can sometimes be guilt producing and she punishes herself by turning from sex. Medications for diabetes or high blood pressure also affect sexual drive.

Preoccupation with the physical is certainly not the answer. "The harder we try to worse it goes," is the common lament of that approach. Tracking one's own performance, for young or old, makes for anxiety which makes people avoid situations formerly associated with intimacy. But periods of abstinence may in fact increase the problem by lowering the usual level of testosterone (which apparently rises in the male after ejaculation). So a vicious circle, that causes what it fears, is put in motion.

More attention to the erotic, where the sexual and spiritual are drawn together, is the answer. Romance can be the form sex takes again after sixty. Romance is humanized, and needs no ulterior reason to be justified. Earlier in life, romance may be what the man is willing to undergo to get sex, while the woman accepts sex to get what she really wants—romance. In youth they may have felt that they were swept away by the urgency of their feelings. Now sex can be something they decide to do. When the urgency of youth has gone, the richness of love has not necessarily gone with it. While carrying less surprise it may yield more sustained wonder. One's life forces are not equivalent to the amount of ejaculate or juiciness. One learns to look for the sign of fuller life for this stage of human growth. The body is not so wasteful as before, but the spirit grows more generous. One looks for the kind of sexual situation that meets one's emotional needs. The process, not the goal, is the goal. Contrasting with this mature attitude is that of the instrumental use of sex: "What is the point if it doesn't lead anywhere?" It is possible for people to excommunicate themselves from their sensual lives as they enter spiritual awareness, just as some excommunicated themselves from a spiritual life when they began their sexual activity. But they can also be reborn sexually. They can come to understand the spiritual truth about the human journey through living fully the fascination and sometimes terror of the sexual life. No amount of education can guarantee it free of sin, but neither is it without grace. Its lifelong shifts and challenges are opportunities for fuller growth in the spirit. The story of human intimacy is told in a no less physical but new way: holding hands, sleeping, cooking, playing together. More silence, but not less communication takes place because of the fact that most of the words have been said at least once.

Sex, which earlier was used as a means to another end, can become more important as personal expression in later life. No longer is there the same agenda, with its drive for self-improvement, its sacrifice for future fulfillment. Finally separated from parents and parenting, the things which caused lack of desire (fear of inadequacy, guilt, self-blame) may have been overcome because the couple can finally talk about all the things that were so fearsome or stood in line behind daily emergencies. The man has proved already what he needs to prove, or has accepted his situation, and is ready to indulge his need for more intimacy; the woman has achieved the self-confidence that makes her more assertive and more interesting. They can invent a more equal relationship, more erotic while less genital, with more cuddling and holding and cherishing. When they come to terms with own priorities and with uniqueness of what they have, they may find renewed intimacy and even better sexual interaction.

The virtue of old age is wisdom. That is often mistaken for prudence which is (ought to be) the virtue of youth. Wisdom urges to daring because one knows one's own and the hearts of others and knows God's heart as without wrath. Research suggests that there is no upper limit to the age at which a woman can experience orgasm, even the first of her life. But why try to expand oneself at this age? Is it not to make a fool of oneself? To one who has continued to value the integration of sexuality into the whole of life, it is no more humiliating a desire or ridiculous a posture than learning a new language or beginning an exercise program. One way of looking at wisdom, and at the last third of life as the time for its ripening, is to see wisdom's task as the development of that which is not yet complete. Wisdom makes way for the good, not only in what is, but in what has not yet been accomplished. Withdrawing passively from life may not be a sign of great virtue; it may rather suggest the hope of some people that if they have never really lived, they may never have to die. "I feel like I'm just discovering a whole new dimension of life," said a seventy-two-year-old student. To continue to live fully in the face of the mixed feelings about age, sex, and mortality and their interrelationships may be the greatest sign of wisdom in the elderly.

Sometimes people need a guide through this territory of the spirit, for our time is unique in the number of people able to reach healthy old age. A new challenge calls new ministries into the field. The ministry of spiritual direction took its historic shape as a service of guidance through crises. When people are in time of danger, precisely danger of interpreting the good as evil and the evil as good, they need a guide who has been there before and found it a path that leads to God. Those who have come through more narrow straits more successfully whole should make the best mentors for others.

Leadership studies have showed that people who form important one-to-one relationships are able to accelerate and intensify their development. That has been dramatically shown in people otherwise apparently destined for a mediocre career. Mentors take risks with people. They bet initially on talent they perceive in younger people. Mentors also risk emotional involvement in working closely with their juniors. The risks do not always "pay off," but the willingness to take them appears crucial in developing leaders. What has, however, been the condition for such relationships, what has provided the psychological readiness of an individual to benefit from an intensive relationship, depends upon some experience in life that forces the individual to turn inward.[11]

In the traditional stories of spiritual growth, guidance is sought particularly when people are moving from structured forms of prayer to more inward and receptive ways of praying. In all the crises of adult sexual development as in spiritual life, some disciplines by which the turn inward is accomplished are important. Interiorization is a spiritual process. It is a universal challenge of mid-life, but it is experienced differently, even uniquely, by individual persons. Daily routines should be recovered or newly established to make room for reflection. The growing edges of the person need nourishment, and she wants to express gratitude for all that has happened.

These periods of solitude and meditation at the same time provide the occasion and motivation to reach out to others. The revival of spiritual direction has raised the issue of discernment, not just to discern movements in the personal lives of individuals but also spiritually significant developments in society. Potential mentors, persons in later life, need a link not just with a spiritual guide but with a community as a resourceful point where the contemplative or active dimensions of our lives can be nourished and strengthened.

The rhythms of the spiritual life can be discovered in the physical. Solitude provides the opportunity to experience a new sense of unity with a wider horizon than was possible with the agitation and demands accompanying earlier stages. You find the one you love in everything, where earlier you tried (and sometimes succeeded) to find everything in him. As Etty Hillesum put it: "You huddle in the corner on the floor in the room of the man you love and darn his socks and at the same time you are sitting by the shore of a mighty ocean so transparent that you can see to the bottom."[12] The point, in summary, is made best of all by John S. Dunne. "What comes to light in the spiritual adventure is the heart's desire. It proves to be a desire for relatedness. As I come to know my own heart, I come to know the hearts of others and even the heart of God."[13]

FOCAL POINTS:

By the term "sex" is indicated the range of possible physical expressions of intimate relation in a life which has progressed through all its stages of development.

"Love" refers to the dynamic that moves anything toward its highest fulfillment. Love of any kind is continuous with the love of God (subjective: God's love for others, and objective: the love of others for God). To speak of differences of degree of love makes more sense than to speak of differences of kinds of love.

The relationship of love to sex in the various stages of development is neither simple identity (one cannot exist without the other) nor simple opposition (one replaces the other to exist). It is sacramental (through sex, human love is made visible and intelligible; through love sex is brought to its own completion). Moreover, through the sacramentality of embodied love, divine love is made present and active.

The holiness of sexual life consists in the lovers' effort to co-work with the Spirit who moves them. That work is Christ's work of reconciliation, which includes and goes beyond personal development toward the improvement of the world.

4

Cycles of Change

Human time does not turn in a circle; it runs ahead in a straight line. That is why man cannot be happy: happiness is the longing for repetition.
Milan Kundera, *The Unbearable Lightness of Being*

Between the hammers lives on our heart, as between the teeth the tongue, which, nevertheless, remains the bestower of praise.
Rainer Maria Rilke, *Duino Elegies* 9

Each stage of life is unique and has a special task that is to be fulfilled in the next stage and become firmly integrated there. The spiritual problem this presents for the individual is that of letting-go. Despite the desire to do so, one should not try to hold on to a stage that is passing. But this tendency also presents a problem for the theologian, whose task it is to work out the differences that each time of life entails in one's relationship to the truth and the demands of love. Youth does not yet understand sacrifice, compromise, or moral failure. People in the prime of life do not understand indifference or detachment. Those who are older, and whose ideas have grown old with them, do not have an easy time believing that things are as good as they were in their youth. When such existential observations are ignored, there is likely to be a view of the demands of the spiritual life that is static and legalistic. Not only is the developmental character of moral maturation ignored, but hope that waits for the Spirit is absent. Deeper insight into the personal life journey acknowledges that there are repeated cycles of change, and that these, to some extent at least, can be recognized and predicted.

Integration is accomplished in living. Thinking separates; living produces the most unlikely connections. Trying to think about something from two points of view promotes dualism, for then considering bodiliness, sexuality, even spirituality distances them from the thinking subject. The focus in thinking is on distinctions. One aspect, then another, can be analyzed, though like the warp and woof of weaving they are only known as they really can be in the wholeness of the cloth. Unraveling the skeins is a precondition for the weaving but never a substitute for it.

Similarly, the only reason for thinking about sex as a process out there is to become more healthy sexually. In my acting, I am a mystery revealing itself, even to me. Aging, for example, is accepted and put into words only after about a ten-year delay. Words are not themselves part of the process, but they may be catalyst for it, disposing us to commit ourselves with a bit less anxiety to the process of growth. In the process of dialog the mystery capable of being revealed in my sexual experience discloses itself. For some, it tells itself as a born-again story of death and rebirth, for others, a story of continuity and bending without breaking.

What drives the whole process is the desire for God deep in things—eros, as it has been called elsewhere in this book. What that process looks like to the outside is change. I want to discuss in this chapter three designations that are not steps or stages, but are intelligible moments in a spiral of growth. Change, even when we have a clue to its benefits, is difficult. It is like the heart "between the hammers," the tongue "between the teeth." What will certainly express itself at times in lament is destined ultimately for praise. These are moments in cycles of changes, not a straight line of progress, and though we feel and are always immeasurably remote from their goal, the product is personal, spiritual transformation. The worthwhile goal, once again, is inseparable from the process. I believe that this law of experience can be illustrated from stories of developing persons: that sexual-spiritual growth takes place by shedding taboos, accepting ambiguity, and finally, celebrating a new way of being.

SHEDDING TABOOS

Historically, the most potent symbol of the dangerous world of the not-sacred is the human body. The body is dangerous and its secretions, particularly semen and menstrual blood, have been enclosed by taboo to protect the social order.[1] The idea of holiness as order (in contrast to the New Testament concept of holiness as mercy) stresses separateness. Confusion of categories of creation (races, species, roles) is prohibited in the simple sense of right order. Under this heading all the rules of sexual morality protect and preserve holiness. Establishing taboos appears to be a positive effort to organize the social environment. What is viewed as unclean may be disputed, but the fact of a list, written or unwritten, remains.

Yet at the same time, the body is sacred. The origin of ritual, to make something sacred by the removal of taboo, acknowledges this. Rituals of purity and impurity establish certain symbolic patterns in which the dualities we experience (body and spirit, male and female, disease and health, guilt and forgiveness) are related and given meaning. Anthropologists and historians of religion have studied taboo and ritual extensively during the past century. The assumption is widespread that primitive peoples used rituals magically, that is, in a mechanical, instrumental way. In the more advanced religions, the concept of uncleanness did not disappear, even though it was less concerned with physical conditions and signified a more spiritual state of unworthiness. Christ, in the theology of the letter to the Hebrews, performs the final removal of taboo, moving religion to the moral level of love and friendship away from the use of sacrifice for appeasement of a divine "system." When taken to an extreme, this view represents a theory of progress. Religion turns away from the manipulation of a system toward the internalization of morality as the essence of religion.

Mary Douglas is illuminating as she challenges this view of progress, and makes the point that we cannot expect to understand other people's ideas of contagion or uncleanness until we have confronted our own. There is a recurrent theme that the reasons for ancient rites are hygienic, for example, that circumcision makes cleanliness easier in a culture with little water; that the avoidance of pork is due to the dangers of eating it in hot climates. But while these are side benefits, they are not found to be a sufficient explanation. Moses was a spiritual leader, not an "enlightened public health administrator," according to Douglas. The spiritual reason, not the secular ones, is given in the tradition: God's holiness requires it. Often there is an assumption that modern rituals of purification are solidly based on hygiene, whereas earlier peoples' were merely symbolic. Douglas argues that modern society's ideas of uncleanness and pollution are different only in detail. Where there is a notion of pollution and disorder, there is a symbolic system by which order is established and holiness is acknowledged. Systems of taboos accumulate because a conservative bias is built in as time goes on and experiences pile up. Uncomfortable facts which do not fit in are ignored or distorted so that we do not have to dislodge established assumptions. As Douglas points out, we "share with other animals a kind of filtering mechanism which at first only lets in sensations we know how to use."[2] What can we do about this? Can we even experience what does not fit the filter? Is it even possible to break new ground? Can we ever examine the filter itself, so as to see things differently? It makes some people feel physically sick, as if their own being was attacked, to have basic assumptions questioned or overturned.

Some, particularly artists and humorists, are able to force confrontation with "perversions" of preconceived reality, the sort of thing that doesn't fit, that is anomalous. Works of art enable us to see behind the veneer of what is accepted in normal experience. It is not impossible for an individual to revise his own personal assumptions in the face of the real experience of anomalies, for example, the person who comes to know that a friend, whom he already loves and respects, is gay can change his deep-seated attitudes. But cultural norms are public matters. They cannot so easily be subject to revision. So one way that a culture can deal with something that appears to be a threat to order is to label it, for example, homosexuality, as "unnatural." In that way the culture's view of reality is not required to change with the appearance of things that don't fit. Second, the existence of something considered disordered can be physically controlled, for example, killed at birth, as superfluous girl children were in some cultures. Third, its prohibition can be taken as a way of strengthening its opposite, for example, absolute opposition to abortion keeps women in service to family. Fourth, that which does not fit acceptable categories may be labeled dangerous. This solution may often arise as a way of reducing dissonance between individual choices and general interpretations. Examples abound here: the social danger that is implied as the result of working mothers, the AIDS fear as a deterrent to sex, anxiety about touch. The labeling of some things as vaguely dangerous is effective in enforcing conformity. Fifth, they may be incorporated into ritual, thus being integrated symbolically into a larger unifying pattern, for example, the use of sexual intercourse in marriage as a public structure for procreation.

Whether or not we are aware of it, that which is perceived to be "out of place" must be restored to order. Dirt must be excluded if the pattern of cleanliness is to be maintained. This functions according to similar rules for both primitives and moderns. Pollution beliefs serve to uphold the taboos. They provide a kind of impersonal punishment for wrongdoing, thus affording a means of supporting the accepted system of morality. This is especially so when a situation is morally ill defined or when moral principles come into conflict. A concern for pollution can reduce confusion by giving people a focus for concern that is simpler than moral reasoning. When action that is held to be morally wrong does not provoke moral indignation or is not reinforced by practical sanctions, belief in the harmful consequences of a pollution can have the effect of marshalling public opinion on the side of the right.

A young woman religious wrote,

Because facing and expressing anger was, for me, bound up with many taboos, dealing with it was a rather touchy and sensitive process, and I had to move through it slowly and delicately. Consequently, I moved in and out of anger throughout the course of therapy. I dealt with and worked through anger in much the same way I was simultaneously dealing with the sexual issue. I would face it up to a point, then back off in terror and fright, until inner pressure forced me to painfully take it out of the closet once more. . . . It terrified me, and my greatest fear was losing control.[3]

The relationship between taboos and morals is far from straightforward. The whole complex of ideas including pollution and purification become a kind of safety net which allows people to perform what, in terms of social structure, could be high-risk actions. Easy purification enables people to defy with impunity the hard realities of their social system. Ironically, pollution fears can provide independent grounds for breaking the moral code which at one time they worked to support. The social environment consists of lines that may not be crossed without danger to self and others. But it is possible for the structure to become self-defeating. That which we fear can easily become fascinating. Sexual collaboration is by nature fertile, constructive, the common basis of social life. But instead of interdependence and harmony, sexual institutions sometimes provoke rigid separation and violent antagonism. Mary Gordon writes in *Final Payments:* "All the things we don't want to tell people are about sex. Sex separates us from everyone but our partner. . . . What was it about sex that I was most ashamed of: the vulnerability it introduced, or the self-ishness?"[4]

The rules of sex pollution are phrased to control entrances and exits to the body as well as to keep straight the clear lines of the social system. Anthropologists find high sex-pollution fears in primitive social structures where men and women need to be bound to their allotted roles. Where sexual roles are enforced directly, that is, where high male dominance is most likely assured by threat of uninhibited physical violence, sex is likely to be pollution free. One thinks of some rural subcultures or those in which education has not challenged the ethnic acceptance of male domestic violence. When the principle of male dominance is applied to the ordering of social life but is part of an obscure or contradictory system, that is, co-exists with aspects of liberation for women or, more likely, recognizes women's rights as the weaker sex to be more protected from violence than men, then notions of sex pollution are likely to flourish. In some contemporary films, such as *Lethal Weapon,* in which male dominance and unbelievable violence are explicit, there is love and protection for women as more vulnerable, but there is no explicit lovemaking.

Anxieties about sex are often transferred from body to food, which also passes the body's boundaries. It may represent a social system at war with itself. This may throw some light on the exaggerated importance attached to virginity in the early centuries of Christianity and to fasting in the medieval period. The primitive church of the Acts, in its treatment of women, was setting a standard of freedom and equality which was against the traditional Jewish custom of subordination of women. Mary Douglas's analysis follows:

> In its effort to create a new society which would be free, unbounded and without coercion or contradiction, it was no doubt necessary to establish a new set of positive values. The idea that virginity had a special positive value was bound to fall on good soil in a small persecuted minority group. . . . The idea of woman as the Old Eve, together with fears of sex pollution, belongs with a certain specific type of social organization. If this social order has to be changed, the Second Eve, a virgin source of redemption crushing evil underfoot is a potent new symbol to present.[5]

Restrictive rules governing the use of sex give visible public recognition of the power and danger of sex. In *Final Payments,* Isabel is nineteen when her father finds her and her boyfriend in bed together:

> But after it happened—David weeping, unable to move, my father shouting outside the door, "get out of here and never come back!"—I did not see him again. . . ."You will never see her again," he said. "You have ruined her life. You have ruined mine. Never come near us again." . . . It must have disappointed him that for my act there was no clear punishment. So he had to invent one: the stoppage of his brain, the failure of his own body as a result of the pleasure of mine. . . . My father's discovery of me that day ensured that no man would ever enter my life in any but a professional capacity. . . . I would remain intact.

Years later, Isabel reflects, "my sex had brought disaster with it. My sex was infecting; my sex was a disease. But now I could make up for it. All that sorrow had come about because I had been selfish, because I had wanted too much."[6]

Purity is a symbol, but when it is lived rigidly it is the enemy of change, of ambiguity and compromise. Most people would feel safer if our experience could be forever set and fixed in forms whose consequences were known and controllable. The yearning for rigidity is not unusual. When we have hard lines and clear concepts, we have to make a choice: either to exclude the realities that don't fit those concepts or blind ourselves to the inadequacy of the concepts.

But life will not forever fit time-bound concepts. The quest for purity in the midst of life creates problems and some curious solutions. One is to enjoy purity at second hand, that is to have professional virgins satisfy the felt need for sexual continence. Another is to claim superior purity, but to allow it to be more rhetorical than literal. Says Douglas, "Whenever a strict pattern of purity is imposed on our lives it is either highly uncomfortable or it leads into contradiction if closely followed, or it leads to hypocrisy."[7] When something is denied or regretted in human nature it is not thereby removed. It continues to demand attention. Life is in the body; it cannot be rejected outright.

> It came to me that life was monstrous: what you loved you were always in danger of losing. The greatest love meant only, finally, the greatest danger. That was life; life was monstrous. But it was life I wanted. . . . life and loss.[8]

It is one of the functions of religion, its sacralizing function, to find some ultimate way of affirming that which has been rejected as "dirty and polluting." If it is to be life-producing and creative in the coming age, religion has to find a way to let sexuality and spirituality come into connection as ritual. There are some things we cannot experience in any other way. To restore to unity all human experience and to overcome distinctions and separations is an effect of ritual, for it modifies experience in expressing it. A liturgy of "perfection" reinforces the separations; a liturgy of "mercy" expresses the connections. As they were theologizing after his departure, the primitive Christians saw Jesus as the dividing line. In him, the divine and human, life and death, blood and food, love and justice—all the things previously kept apart—are celebrated together. Here is the end of taboo and the beginning of ambiguity in an extreme and concentrated form, proclaimed as the source of our salvation.

The existence of taboo symbolizes both danger and power. The shedding of taboo, while it is destructive to existing patterns, also has potentiality. By eliminating self-conscious reflection on the sexual, it was separated from the life of holiness offered for people's contemplation. By the negative prohibitions, the outlines of the ideal social order were traced and retraced. Moral growth must mean a change in one's position toward these. Progress means differentiation. Teilhard de Chardin, in fact, developed the theme that the movement of evolution has been toward ever-increasing complexification and self-awareness. And Joseph Campbell has offered the insight contained in the parable, originally from Nietzsche, which shows human spiritual growth as first in the image of the camel, then the lion, and finally the child.

> In the early years of life one is like a camel who lies down to have great burdens loaded upon its back. The heavier the loads it learns to

carry, the greater will be its power later. In the prime of life, a person is like a lion who goes into the desert to kill the dragon. But the dragon is a specific dragon, on each of whose scales is written "Thou shalt!" Only when the dragon of "Thou shalt" has been overcome, can the person go on to the next stage of growth, that in which a child emerges, a child which is like a wheel, "rolling out of its own center."

From the shedding of taboos through the overcoming of legalistic morality to the morality of the heart is the journey taken by the spiritual person. Scrupulosity was a term defined in Catholic moral theology to refer to the obsessive behavior of those who attempt to adhere to every detail of the ritual and moral codes presented to them by authority figures. Because they set themselves the impossible task of rigid conformity to rules, they necessarily fell into sins which produced guilt and the desire to impose even stricter forms of conformity. They became involved in a spiral which led away from the authentic Spirit.

The shedding of taboos is a phenomenon which can be observed when it has been accomplished. It is not something one sets out to do, but something one finds upon reflection to be done. Like discovering one no longer believes in Santa Claus. The loss of the power of taboo has, however, a positive function for the individual. Conscience can then be awakened to a moral sense of individual rights and responsibilities. A student described the experience as follows:

> I think I was probably at a two-year-old stage of sexual development and an unhealthy one at that. I was very comfortable in my legalism so when the bottom fell out, it was total chaos for me. I know now it was a place of growth and acceptance. When I was in that stage, I did sometimes feel like an intern. Since my clinging to rules was so entrenched in me, the ripping away was intensely painful and frightening. There had been a security about being a great rule follower. It made me very self-righteous and arrogant.

The broken taboo can be frightening, but it can also be the signal that an individual is awakening to the realization that his sexuality is his own, not outside and more powerful than himself. As Isabel comes to insight that she has been hiding from life so that she might not suffer the pain of loss, she remembers Jesus' words during the scene of Magdalen anointing his feet:

> But now I understood. What Christ was saying, what he meant, was that the pleasures of that hair, that ointment, must be taken. Because the accidents of death would deprive us soon enough. I knew

now I must open the jar of ointment. I must open my life. . . . But I was not ready. I would have to build my strength.[9]

The deliberate choice to break a habit in one's life is also a different process from the shedding of taboos, though a taboo may have to be shed before one can begin. Deliberately breaking a taboo can even be a way of stopping further growth, as it is possible to be brash enough to break old patterns without being courageous enough to enter the ambiguity of new possibilities. The overturning of taboos without continued growth toward interior responsiveness is disastrous. Conservative voices recognize the seriousness of this far more perceptibly than liberal voices.

For society the shedding of taboos along with growth toward interior spiritual awareness and moral responsiveness functions to promote tolerance. As a widespread phenomenon it may signal a shift from an oversimplified dualistic to a pluralistic mode of conceptualizing the shoulds and oughts of human life. The shedding of taboos, ironically, is a precondition for unity in a pluralist and crowded world.

LIMINALITY

Without taboos, a person is faced with perhaps the most difficult moment in the dynamic of change: the acceptance of ambiguity. As an essential middle stage by which one moves from external certainties, it is the situation of being able to live between the possibilities. Alternatives for future interpretations of oneself, not yet discovered, are multiple and undefined. The acceptance of ambiguity can be correlated to the stage of liminality in initiation rites, a stage named from the image of a novice, standing in the threshold, not yet inside or outside, but on the doorstep. I think sexual growth offers people particularly poignant opportunities to grow from taboo-defined behavior to learning to be serene in the fluidity of dual interpretations of one's own and others' actions and feelings. "Alcoholism was for me," wrote one student, "a way of numbing the pain while I played the various assorted roles that were expected. Alcoholism also helped me find a way out of that relationship. . . . My addiction to alcohol was my spiritual catalyst to reclaiming myself. Now in recovery I am a full-time chemical dependency counselor, a full-time student and a full-time partner."

In our own human body is our deepest experience of ambiguity; it is both me and not me; it is our vehicle of separation as well as connection; it defines our possibilities and our limitations. Through it occur our only and deepest experiences of pleasure and fulfillment, and in it we return over and over to the pain of hunger, frustration, and need. Accepting our bodiliness, not just as good rather than evil, but as the ultimate evidence of the fact that good and evil are two interpretations of the same reality, is the way we learn to accept ambiguity in larger things. It would be easier to accept our bodies as anomalies, in the sense defined by Mary Douglas[10] as something that does not fit in a system, rather than as symbolic of the ambiguity of life. Then we could suppress one pole of the ambiguity and maintain the illusion that we are really of the spirit world, with the body an irrelevant nuisance. Those in passage from one clear way of being to another are treated as both vulnerable and dangerous. Society, wrote Arnold Van Gennep in *Rites of Passage,* is a house with rooms and corridors in which passage from one to another is dangerous.[11] Danger lies in transitional states, simply because transition is neither one state nor the next; it is undefinable. Not only is the person who must pass from one to another in danger himself; he emanates danger to others. In primitive cultures the danger is controlled by ritual which, through rites of initiation, precisely separates him from his old status, segregates him for a time and then publicly declares his entry to his new status. The rituals of segregation are the most dangerous phase of the initiation process. Here the ideas of pollution and purification interact with the theme of death and rebirth. During the marginal period, persons in transition are temporarily outcast. They have no place in society. They are marginal, socially and psychologically. Sometimes they even separate themselves physically, as has been observed in the correlation of increased instances of the disorder known as agoraphobia with menopause, and the appearance of antisocial behavior (stealing, rape, obscenity, outrageous acts) with adolescence. Separation, solitude, are the peculiarly proper expressions of marginal condition. The words of this student capture the heart of that insight: "My choice, to remain celibate for now, did not result as a punishment from God for getting divorced, but rather is a unique time in my life, specifically set aside in order to explore areas of myself including sexuality."

Separateness involves loneliness, not to be regarded as unfortunate but a real and necessary task for the middle moment in the cycle of change. It may not be physical at all but spiritual, an experience of the desert, of inner loneliness, a place between two worlds where one could "walk in oneself and meet no one for hours on end."[12]

Language manifests culturally the level of acceptance of ambiguity that is normative. In some cultures, one is conditioned to value it; in others one has almost to rebel in order to enter an experience of liminality. The human mind needs to construct formulations that are ambiguous in order to express feelings and articulate realities which are too subtle for straightforward informational language. Words like youth and love—and body—recognize this. They are ambiguous. Western intellectual culture since the scientific revolution has disparaged the use of ambiguities at all levels of communication, though it makes possible fiction, humor, and poetry. Students of culture show that such an overvaluing of factual discourse is a unique development in world history. Most premodern cultures have accorded a position of privilege to expression that is intentionally ambiguous. Most of the wisdom literatures of surviving religions are noted for precepts open to multiple interpretation. More attention is paid to the unknown and the undefined when the surface meaning is unclear. A value for truth as mystery, such a theology assumes, might even provide a context in which obscurity is preferable to that which is clear. The point is that ambiguity does not characterize ignorance, or lack of knowledge, but wisdom, love for that which is larger than what can be known by empirical means. A student described her experience in these words:

> Today the darkness of addiction is still as clear as it was four years ago when I stepped off the plane in Minneapolis to undergo my third primary treatment for alcoholism. The days, then, seemed gray and cold and the ground was covered with ice. . . . In the course of the last treatment, something outside clicked. A counselor said, "In order to gain control, sometimes we have to give up control." These words and that moment seemed to freeze in time. I could not shake them from my thoughts nor could I understand them. Then, it was as if there was a light; a spiritual moment, for the words and their meaning became vividly clear. In the past four years, I have come to believe that in the darkest of moments, in the depths of despair, often it is the simplest of truths that shall spark the lights and that of the spiritual moments.

Double entendre is one form of speech in which ambiguity is recognized as intrinsic to sexual existence. People who are not truly poets write poetry when they are in the grasp of romantic love. It is language that "dances around" the issue—of attraction or invitation—in a variety of ways without having to move to decision or confrontation. That would stop the process.

The connection of sexuality, food, and liminality is illustrated in an interesting way by some recent analysis of women's food disorders, apparently a new phenomenon at least in its extent in our time. A social theorist, Brian Turner observes that it is *anorexia nervosa* which most dramatically expresses the ambiguities of female gender in contemporary Western societies: "the onset of anorexia is situated in a conflict over dependence and autonomy in the relationship between mother and daughter. In this context, the refusal to eat, however secretly that refusal is pursued, is an act of rebellion which breaks the social bonds created by nurturing."[13] Anorexia thus transforms a previously compliant "good girl" into a naughty but determined rebel. The rebellion is of course primarily a symbolic gesture which cuts off the nurturing bond which the girl has felt to be as bondage. So anorexia involves a power struggle within the family over food. The girl's search for individuation and autonomy is fought out over her own body and the closeness associated with the family table. This interpretation in some ways departs from those which see food disorders in women as the consequence of patriarchal values forcing unworkable norms of beauty on women. Both approaches, however, recognize them as related to the general position of women in society. Agoraphobia and anorexia are expressive of the anxiety of closeness. The agoraphobic, according to Brian Turner, suffers from protective patriarchy; the anorexic from the too-protective parent in the too-tight family circle. Obesity represents another variation on the theme. Producing in one's own body a transformation that one has not chosen yet cannot reject is irrational. But the rejection of enforced values regarding what is rational is precisely what is at stake. When a woman takes control of what she looks like, she has made a symbolic statement against the system that is perceived to dominate. The obese woman is not simply fat; she is literally "out of control." As Thomas Szasz views it, "Addiction, obesity, starvation are political problems, not psychiatric: each condenses and expresses a contest between the individual and some other person or persons in his environment over the control of the individual's body."[14]

The concept of ambiguity can illumine a new, dimly understood way of being by allowing an individual to try on various modes without being socially bound to them. It can "open the mind" of the culture to what it might not have been able to conceive before. Sex and mysticism both involve a kind of surrender to a sense of what has never been known before. "A more inclusive sense of reality, a sense of mystery, and the experience of oneness that accompanies release of tension—these are the attributes of mysticism. Ambiguity is par excellence the handmaid of mysticism, a type of cognitive orientation primarily concerned with the meaning of life and of the world."[15]

American culture may be a chilly environment for both sexual and spiritual life because of its scientific and pragmatic orientations. Donald Levine argues that a strong practical orientation to dominate nature and an intellectual orientation toward gaining cognitive mastery over the world contributed to the American aversion toward ambiguity.[16] Unambiguous language and specific roles are indispensable for any highly developed technological society. Still, the inner life cannot be replaced or expedited by efficiency. Acceptance of ambiguity marks the necessary step in a change that deepens a person's inner life and expands her social life beyond previously imagined conceptions. As a student wrote,

Personally, I am in the state of liminality, or experimentation—trying to find a way to fit my spirituality into a tradition that I feel comfortable with and can celebrate with others. I am still having real problems with my inability to integrate my past with the present in hopes of finding an acceptable outlet for my new-found spiritual life.

The acceptance of ambiguity serves to increase the options a person can imagine. That, in contrast to a frenetic search for additional opportunities to act out a single option, is growth toward freedom. In her Journal, Etty Hillesum wrote, "And I know for certain there will be continuity between the life I have led and the life about to begin. Because my life is increasingly an inner one and the outer setting matters less and less."[17]

When the main character in the film *Shirley Valentine*, a middle-aged woman who followed an uncharacteristic impulse to vacation in Greece, says in farewell to her lover of one day: "I fell in love with, not you, but the possibility of living," she is reflecting the newness that comes from liminality. Actually she may now be able to love her husband with new ardor because she is once again situated in the rushing flow of life. She had been numb with routine and compromise. As a student put it, "As I journey, I see myself moving from a row boat to a sail boat. The integration of my sexuality and my spirituality will be dynamite."

How does this function get carried out in the practical order? Fantasy is one way, less expensive and inconvenient than a trip to Greece. Fantasy expresses the sexual dynamic in an "immaterial" mode. It can be a safety valve. It allows the person self-knowledge without the interaction of physical bodies. It protects the person and his potential partner from prematurely acting out the sexual impulse when the phenomenon of arousal is still not integrated into the person as moral agent.

Fantasy, as the ability to inhabit an image without acting it out, can also be a platform for social criticism and change. Art and drama do this; even explicit erotic literature can be so if it remains in the timeless, placeless fantasy world. When it moves out into the real world, as comment on or cause of real relations in the real world, it loses its function of safety valve, because it is no longer a playground of the imagination. Through the medium of fantasy the obsessive character of sexual impulses can be diffused. As one entertains something imaginatively, one can regain the freedom to choose it as a perma-nent part of one's identity or not. "I could do that . . . but I won't!"

The disequilibrium brought about by transitions can take many forms: boredom, illness, confusion, dissatisfaction. Some people experience depres-sion, which as we are told, is often anger turned inward. To find a way to ventilate it without lashing out indiscriminately at systems and institutions, or turning it back on oneself in a destructive way is important for releasing the energy of anger toward change.

With all its effectiveness in bringing about creative change in an individual and in her relation to a community, ambiguity has its limits. As a state of no commitments, it must be linked to a willingness and an ability to press toward ending ambiguity at appropriate moments. Liminality is a stage between states, not a state in which to live, a state of no commitments.

A professional woman wrote as follows about her own experience:

> For the first 25 years of my life, as sensually as I related to life around me, I denied myself the opportunity to explore my sexuality. There were perhaps several reasons for this, the most significant being my growing awareness of my attractions to my girlfriends instead of my boyfriends. Oh, how I wished I could have been like Peter Pan, never grow up and never have to deal with this. In part my denials were built on the fear of total rejection for being so different. I can honestly say there has never been a doubt in my mind in terms of my sexual preference. The only doubts were based on how to survive in a predominately heterosexual world and how would I discover other women with the same intentions?

There is a time for ambiguity and a time for singleness of mind and firmness of will. To be able to express personal concerns to another is a step toward resolution of those concerns. Attempting to articulate one's insights in a manner lucid enough for another to understand, a person must present one factor at a time in some comprehensible order, a process that helps to resolve the confusion. It leads to renaming, not only in one's self-awareness, but creates in the real world new interpersonal bonds, which themselves become part of the new and viable self-image. The woman quoted above continues, "I shared my story with my two closest friends, one who I then found out was also gay, and the other who was totally accepting. Both have remained my close friends. So much for the fear of rejection."

RENAMING

Some change involves the creation of adoption of a new role or self-image; at other times it requires rather a shift in the relations between existing elements. "I'm glad I had to struggle because I am more alive and free than I ever dreamed I could be," said a middle-aged nun. The ideal of perfect, static integration is not what is envisioned here. That is so impossible in the conditions of life before death that to urge it upon people would prove an obstacle rather than an inspiration. What is within our power, however, is to claim the highest possible significance for our moments of self-articulation. The price of such moments of insight is an attentiveness and loyalty to the real things and relationships that immediately surround us. Its reward is the habit of celebrating what is. On the other hand, insight into what is newly discovered is precluded by some sort of illusion that there can be a permanently satisfying grasp of things. By reflection we can reconcile ourselves with our limitations, and gain at least some insight into how ultimately unified are our namings of life and death, sorrow and joy, body and spirit. When Penelope Washbourn wrote the following lines I believe she was reaching for the notions of authenticity and integration:

> I don't often think of my body as an organic reality intimately connected with everything around it. I think of it more as a separate body with boundaries. My problem is to find the connections again, to find the other without losing myself. That's the fear, fear of risking too much of myself, fear of trusting. That fear keeps my neck muscles tense, keeps me from sexual fulfillment. It will keep me finally from being able to die in peace. [18]

The more one changes the less one tries to fit an ideal. No pattern or guide but a series of proposals; that's what namings are. The person who celebrates arrival at a preset goal is as happily surprised as anyone to find out where her next step leads. Actually we are able to name only in retrospect. We move into the future glancing into the rear-view mirror. The perspective is not that of a straight line, but of a spiral. Renaming puts one experientially at the heart of the paschal mystery. Everything, including prayer and sexual excitement, falls apart and needs to be reconstructed. This is the process of transformation. The personal task of undertaking change again and again is possible when one can articulate with confidence a newly discovered aspect of self without the illusion of permanence. Love is never having to say always. Love is knowing that "unless one is born anew, he cannot see the kingdom of God" (John 3:3). Jesus continues, "Do not marvel that I said to you, 'You must be born anew.' The wind blows where it wills and you hear the sound of it, but you do not know whence it comes or whither it goes; so it is with everyone who is born of the Spirit" (3:7–8).

A woman of forty-something wrote:

> As I read my Journal, I saw a definite pattern emerging. There would be a crisis period between my husband and me every three to four weeks. It was quite a revelation. . . . As I thought about it, I knew I didn't want

to continue this game. The archaic rules no longer made any sense to me, and, in addition, I was getting tired of "band-aid" sex. . . . We talked, and agreed that we would work harder on communication, but my sense is that I am separated internally no matter where my body is. Through my soul-searching, although I know that I am a sexual person, for right now, genital sex is not for me.

Sexual and spiritual potential can remain undeveloped because people play one role too intensely and frequently. Only by moving out of this role and developing self-worth is an identity reclaimed. People can undermine and sabotage themselves, turning what ought to be success into failure. When they repeatedly place themselves in situations or with people where they will be mistreated, used or abused, they are demonstrating lack of personal power. We don't use the personal power we have when we excuse ourselves from change or improvement because of a vague sense of what we "are" that is unchangeable, for example, "shy" as used to explain away loneliness and unhappiness. In a sense our attitudes about ourselves are ourselves, with or without the strength to make changes. Life itself sometimes forces us to make changes. Sometimes stories from the lives of others, showing their willing use of personal power, can do the same thing:

> I have just celebrated three years sobriety in March. This has done wonders for my self-esteem. I will not tolerate abuse from anyone any longer. I can't. I can feel it. My divorce was the second best thing that ever happened to me. I feel a special power now because I am no longer afraid of him. He has no power over me. I have become a superb limit setter. The damage from the rapes continues to trouble me, but at least I am now entertaining the thought of dating again. It took me almost two years to get over that after the divorce. . . . This has caused me to realize that I have more strength and courage than I've ever given myself credit for.

The third moment in the cycle of change, whether called renaming, celebration, or transformation, is the result of a personal healing process in which we accept ourselves, without trying to split off those parts that we find unworthy. In that reintegration we transcend our previous experience of ourselves and increase our capacity to be centered persons.

FOCAL POINTS:
Men and women are open, dynamic beings capable of growth and advancement.
Taboos excite in the breaking, not in the keeping; therefore they are useless in the

Sexuality and Spiritual Growth

effort to produce responsible sexual action, that is, action in conformity with community standards, yet productive of personal spiritual growth.

The phenomenon of overspecialization is able to explain some of the unconventional outlets for sexual energy that society has found it necessary to reject. Acceptance of ambiguity with regard to human sexuality, especially at certain stages of development, can extend the range of options for individuals without endangering others.

A theology of grace locates God's action where "options are maximized." By contrast, sin is becoming curved in upon oneself, in fear and refusal to change, and in refusal of forgiveness.

5

⚘

Theology of Spirit

Every scribe who is learned in the reign of God is like the head of a household who can bring from his store both the new and the old.
Matthew 13:46

Send out a crier, she says

I want to talk to the people.
Listen   Listen   while you are walking
All is upon the earth and all is sacred.
Meridel LeSueur, "Behold This and always love it"

Love Letter

I hate you, God.
Love, Madeleine

Madeleine L'Engle, *The Irrational Season*

Life-talk is essential for God-talk. Exploring the implications of human sexual self-understanding is just as important for right understanding of theology today as knowing the doctrine of the past (orthodoxy) or following the right path of gospel living (orthopraxis). Reflection is the step most often missing between action and doctrine. When that happens, the theology, not the life, is rendered invalid. If theology and life are not in dialog, life becomes mute and theology turns deaf.

I think two areas in particular will be affected by more systematic reflection on sexual life in the light of faith. They are the doctrine of God, especially as a theology of the Holy Spirit, and the theology that underlies moral decision-making. I would like to call this a theology of morality, to suggest that it is more foundational than applied.

DOCTRINE OF GOD

In all authentic expression of sexual relation a mystery of immanence and transcendence is experienced that can be the source of thematic reflection about ultimate mystery. "Everyone who belongs to my life is far and near, it seems, as God is far and near, as I myself am far and near, in my presence of mind."[1]

Extended reflection upon sexuality impresses upon one that it combines both power and surrender, creation and kenosis, healing and destruction. This synthesis of opposites, as experienced in a human sexual life, is a possible source of new images of God. Not only is the compassionate face of God, the face of the Mother of Mercy, recognized in the intimate moments of life; also the absence of God, who takes away as well as gives, is known. The tension between the two aspects of one Reality is precisely what catapults us into Mystery. As is suggested in the quote from Madeleine L'Engle, Love and hate are not opposites: "God sometimes withdraws. He has not answered my knock for a long time and this is beginning to make me angry. Why isn't he there when I need him so desperately? So I wrote another Love Letter:" And it continues as above, I hate you . . . love you. . . .[2]

These two ways of seeing persons—their distance (transcendence) and their nearness (immanence), both knowable in their presence—are the experiential roots of a theology of God. In turn, the models of God that are developed out of those experiences (and one pole is usually stronger than another in any one particular climate or culture) become the theological roots of a representative spirituality. Awareness of God as a mystery greater than any human being and impossible to command is the experience of transcendence. What resists us in another, his freedom, her otherness, is a parable of God's transcendence. "The parable," writes John Dunne, "is human love" which is a "shape taken by the love of God."[3] At times we become aware of being addressed by that God, and the Other becomes the "heart's desire," a longing for presence that ruins our peace of mind. Consciousness of God being near gives rise to concepts of revelation, when the veils of the ineffable mystery are removed and what was hidden becomes momentarily clear and communicable. The relationship between theology and spirituality is also exemplified here. A desire to know God (spirituality) is accompanied and perhaps preceded by the desire to know about God (theology).

There is a third experience of paradox that people know from sexual relationships that is also theologically formulated. As such, it in turn roots spirituality. It is the experience of searching for a relationship—human longing, but also and without any pattern, the comparable experience of having been sought out by the other without any effort or worthiness of our own. Love is hard work; love is a gift. First we know God's gracious action toward us; then comes our response (which looks to us like initiative). "Prayer is the breath of the soul as air is the natural breath of the body. We breathe spiritually by the Holy Spirit. You cannot say a single word of prayer from your whole heart without the Holy Spirit."[4] The quest for God, and the sense of having been found by God's initiative alone, coinhere in the theology of grace and the dynamic of the spiritual life.

"I seek for God that he may find me," writes Madeleine L'Engle,

> because I have learned, empirically, that this is how it works. I seek: he finds. The continual seeking is the expression of hope for a creator great enough to care for every particular atom and sub-atom of his creation, from the greatest galaxy to the smallest farandolae. Because of my particular background I see the coming together of macrocosm and microcosm in the Eucharist, and I call this Creator: God, Father; but no human being has ever called him by his real name, which is great and terrible and unknown, and not to be uttered by mortal man.[5]

Christian theology has named this unknown "Trinity," putting into that symbolic word the perception that the One known must be Relational. The doctrine of God as personal required the model of God as relational. Christians come to think about this God as already in relationship with human being, that is, in Christ. As in relation to history, God is named and encountered as Spirit, a word that is less an affirmation of what is known about God than an assertion about words' inability to contain the Holy Mystery.

Sometimes a failure in spiritual life (a failure in the integration of sensual life with Spirit) can be traced to half-true, but too-clear theological formulations. How people understand God intellectually determines in part whether they accept or reject a relationship with God. So it is worth probing whether theological insight might serve as a path to spiritual awareness. Theological models of God also play a prophetic role. They organize life according to what they reveal as symbols of ultimate value. Since the symbol is always transcended by the reality, that is, it is never univocal, it needs to be critiqued in terms of the personal and social forms that it brings to expression. The biblical reflection on God as covenantal partner, as in Hosea, proceeds from human analogies to affirmations about divine fidelity. To go the other direction: from doctrinal assumptions about God to affirmations about normative forms of human experience is, as Theodore Mackin points out,[6] an extremely precarious use of analogy. So not only parenting love, or procreative marital love, can be appropriate symbolic material; so can be lesbian and gay love; so is friendship. So is work that loves the earth and produces for it. These models play a prophetic role. Appeal to a divine example of normative love cannot be an excuse for the institutionalized support of some forms of relationship arbitrarily over others. No longer should the model of God as personal become the reason for the privatization of the gospel, so that the work of the inner life is separated from the work of social restructuring in the world. The symbol is always transcended by the reality, yet brings aspects of it to expression. The human reality of love also always transcends our expressions of it, which is why its continuity with the divine can be, finally, affirmed.

> The longing of the heart is that very love [of God]. If it does come from God and go to God, if it is "of God," even God's own love in us, then our longing is its own requital, our prayer is its own answer. Then our life is about the love of God.[7]

Two things are widely affirmed about the Holy Spirit. She is Love and She is the Spirit of Christ. Because of the predominance of Christology in the development of Christian theology from the earliest days, the Spirit as Spirit of Christ is often all that is known. To enter ritually into Christ's passion and mission in the world, that is, to enter the church, one must come to share the life of that Spirit. Sometimes, though, the manner in which the relation between Christ and Spirit has been formulated in the West leads to an impression that the Spirit is only instrumental—a means to the end which is Christ. But St. Thomas wrote: "The Holy Spirit is identically the same in Christ and in ourselves."[8]

That is unequivocal. Our life in the Spirit is its own reality, its own reason for being, not just transition to mystical or institutional identification with Christ. To the extent that our Christology is not explicitly cognizant of the role of the Holy Spirit, not just in Jesus but between members of the community of faith, it is inadequate. The Scriptures show the Spirit as "bringing to remembrance" what Jesus has said (John 14:26), and "bearing witness" to Jesus (15:26). She is generous not fearful, guiding us into the whole truth (6:13). The Spirit does this precisely in history, during the time of Jesus' bodily absence. How? As the Spirit of truth, she is with the disciples and in them forever in order to bear witness with them to Christ and his work (15:26–27) and to celebrate with them the coming in fullness of what Jesus began (Rev. 22:17). As the Paraclete, the Spirit also acts as advocate for those who walk in the truth, strengthening and reassuring them against the opposing forces. The Spirit's help is never absent when persons who believe in her pass through a struggle with the dark world from which the Spirit is excluded. This world is not the specifically human world of sexual relation. The biblical terms "the world" and "the flesh" are ambiguous, requiring reinterpretation in succeeding ages. John Cassian points out that the word *flesh* is used in the Scriptures with many different meanings: sometimes it stands for the whole person, sometimes for humanity as sinful, sometimes for sins themselves, but it may also mean simply blood relationship. Therefore inquiry into the context is important before it is assumed the reader understands the meaning of a text. As St. Isaac of Syria cautioned his monks: "When you hear that it is necessary to withdraw from the world, to leave the world, to purify yourself from all that belongs to the world, you must first learn and understand the term 'world' not in its normal everyday use, but in its purely interior meaning."9

In case one should think that normal people were incapable of such exercises in hermeneutics, he should consider how commonplace, in ordinary morality on the uses of money and violence, in ethics of business and war, has discerning such "an interior meaning" become. The acceptable human use of riches and the appropriate use of power are distinguishable from the evil uses of these things. So too, the Scriptures would bear, should be the use of sex. Those who think they know categorically what is of the Spirit and what is not are set on their heels by texts such as 1 Corinthians 2:10–11: "the Spirit searches everything, even the depths of God. For what person knows a man's thoughts except the spirit of the man which is in him? So also no one comprehends the thoughts of God except the Spirit of God"; and 2:15: "The spiritual man judges all things, but is himself to be judged by no one."

Experiencing the Spirit

The Scriptures speak of the Spirit, not systematically as in an academic treatise, but in terms of persons' experience. This experience is not reducible to what we are accustomed to call experience in everyday life: in the sense of the raw material of experience, physical contact or empirical knowledge. The experience of the Spirit resembles an awareness not of an object outside us, but of the innermost core of our subjective existence. It may be triggered by outside events but is often written about in spatial images as the inner life or an interior chamber one enters. There is a "place" where the person is present to herself as the subject knowing more or less clearly that she undergoes the many particular "experiences" of everyday life. Etty Hillesum found words to describe the feeling.

> Sometimes when I least expect it, someone suddenly kneels down in some corner of my being. When I'm out walking or just talking to people. And that someone, the one who kneels down, is myself.

And again: "That part of myself, that deepest and richest part in which I repose, is what I call God."10 This center can be forgotten, and with it the sense of wholeness, when a person loses herself in the multiplicity of details of a normal daily routine. But it is not truly lost; it only remains hidden behind the more superficial encounters. The experience of the Spirit, writes Rahner, "is not to be rejected out of hand as non-existent, merely because—like the self-givenness of the human individual—it is liable to be overlooked in all specific experience."[11]

So one should not look for the experience of "the Spirit" as a specific experience, but as the ground of all experience. The problem with such an explanation for most of us is that it is so easy to doubt its possibility. It sounds like wishful thinking and circular reasoning. To expect to have the same sense of immediacy from the presence of the Spirit as one has of warmth and heightened excitement over the nearness of an attractive partner is, upon examination, absurd. We know of other genuine experiences which are not registered in material terms nor even capable of being verbalized: experiences such as that of freedom or of hostility or of genuine fortuity.

> If a love is to be unforgettable, fortuities must immediately start fluttering down to it like birds to Francis of Assisi's shoulders. . . . It may well be those few fortuities . . . which set her love in motion and provided her with a source of energy she had not yet exhausted at the end of her days. . . . it is right to chide a man for being blind to such coincidences in his daily life. For he thereby deprives his life of a dimension of beauty.[12]

It goes without saying that people have and continue to report the immediate experience of illumination or union with God. That this experience is the experience of the Holy Spirit is obscured by the great variety of cultural images and theological assumptions in which it has been cast. These can serve to confuse us as well as compel our belief. In itself, the cultural gap should not render the experience incredible, but for many it does. It is not so much the religious core as the cultural trappings that put us off. God revealing her gracious presence in the form of a woman is not that hard to believe; the weeping statue of the virgin, for most of us, is. God as love, continuity in the forms of love? No problem, conceptually. But God as sexual love in a sex-negative culture? Blasphemy and obscenity. Credible testimony of their experience of the Spirit in sexual experience has not been offered by people, but is it surprising? Theologians have stressed the extraordinary, reserved nature of mystical phenomena. Is it any wonder that the sexually active should treat immediate experience of God as something that does not concern them?

Isolated from peripheral phenomena such as visions and ecstacies, the core experience of the liberating power of grace is more frequent than we might otherwise think. That experience of the Spirit is offered to us, though we usually overlook it in the pursuit of our everyday agenda; perhaps we repress it and do not take it seriously enough. Each individual knowing and wanting is open to the Mystery, what Karl Rahner calls the "horizon," that embraces it. If one is irritated by this and prefers to act as if human things are "nothing but" what is delivered by the routine of everyday life, he works against his own ultimate being. As Walter Kasper expresses it, "theonomy brings autonomy to fulfilment as autonomy. The greater the unity with God, the greater the freedom of the human being."[13] Translating this idea, one could say: the Spirit brings the sexual to fulfillment *as sexual*. The unconditional dependence on God as the origin and goal of human life does not exclude human autonomy. On the contrary, it sets it free. One's depths calling to the depths of the Spirit is what makes possible all ordinary calling and responding, it does not make it extraordinary. Etty Hillesum found herself coining a word to adequately describe this phenomenon, experienced in the process of listening to another in friendship. In Dutch, the term is *hinein-houken*. "And if I say that I hearken, it is really God who hearkens inside me. The most essential and the deepest in me hearkening unto the most essential and the deepest in the other. God to God."[14]

With an "add-on" mentality in which there is no sacred dimension but only an unending series of finite things, we tend to think of awareness of God as some kind of extra luxury which some special people are given, but as Karl Rahner shows through his analysis of the core of human transcendence, the presence of God is the very condition without which no other presence could be encountered. God is the You addressed in every "you." Put bluntly, the point is not that it is possible, with effort, to put God in sex; it is that it is impossible to have authentic sex except in God. It is not only our understanding of sex that is at fault, but our assumptions about God.

The experience of God is not, then, a special, particularly unusual encounter with an objective reality, something to be named and classified as one of our daily series of encounters. God is known incomprehensibly in the knowing of all other objects of experience. So Rahner clarifies[15] that when I experience the Spirit it does not look like the Spirit but is the anonymous, unthematic knowing behind the thematic knowledge of the neighbor, the written text, the friend, even one's own face.

> It was not vanity that drew her to the mirror; it was amazement at seeing her own "I." She forgot she was looking at the instrument panel of her body mechanisms; she thought she saw her soul shining through the features of her face. . . . Each time she succeeded was a time of

intoxication: her soul would rise to the surface of her body like a crew charging up from the bowels of a ship, spreading out over the deck, waving at the sky and singing in jubilation. [16]

Images are more luminous than concepts when it comes to spirit. The Spirit is the light in which everything in my world becomes visible, the breath by which all words are spoken to me, the floor around me which supports the spot on which I stand. This common way of experiencing God in everyday life is not challenged or made less credible by a second way in which the Spirit is experienced. When the contours of the normal fail and dissolve, when what we trust no longer holds, when death or crisis or trauma overtake us, then another kind of experience is reported. More typical of the "twice-born" personality, this is what the classical spiritual writers called the negative way, the experience of God when the structures of the routine temporarily crack apart and one is faced with the choices in the darkness. While distinguishable from the first way, these should be seen as two aspects of one and the same experience: the depth is there whether it persists in the midst of the banalities of everyday things or whether it breaks through in moments of crisis. The idea of "composing" such a life is attractive. "Without realizing it, the individual composes his life according to the laws of beauty even in the times of greatest distress." [17]

Examples of such experiences are innumerable. There is the one who discovers she can forgive though it does not take away the pain; she hears through her loss the word of forgiveness from God. Another lets go in trust and hope, and finds that what happens is totally gratuitous, immensely more valuable than his own worth or effort. There is the one who does his duty knowing that no one else can take it from him, and that no one is likely to thank him for it. When beauty or love or pleasure are accepted purely for themselves without calculation, where death in any of its forms is accepted as a leap into the future, the Spirit breaks through. These experiences of the Spirit include the grace of discovering God in all things. They should not be rejected or despised because the events are commonplace or frequent. Not if it is true that the whole composition of life follows the contours of the Spirit.

Yet intentional development of religious consciousness, ritual awareness, meditation and spiritual exercises are also valuable training ground for the discernment of the Spirit. Just as in physical workout the body produces endorphins which improve mood and have been shown to make people more self-confident sexually, so spiritual exercises can afford the opportunity to experience the Spirit more clearly and reflectively. These are catalysts for decisions to integrate the whole of one's existence toward salvation, using those particular spiritual paths that appeal to one in her own unique life story. A great deal of discernment and spiritual practice is necessary to recognize accurately the occasions when a longing for a specific pleasure offered by everyday life is the starting-point rather than a distraction from an ultimate experience of the Spirit. A person needs to learn to recognize, with others, for himself, when a particular experience threatens the synthesis of the Spirit and everyday duties. Tomas, in *The Unbearable Lightness of Being,* knew about these things.

> His love for Tereza was beautiful, but it was also tiring: he had constantly to hide things from her, sham, dissemble, make amends, buck her up, calm her down, give her evidence of his feelings, play the defendant to her jealousy, her suffering and her dreams, feel guilty, make excuses and apologies. Now what was tiring had disappeared and only the beauty remained.[18]

There was the interlude in which he was running from the routine in search of the beauty, and there was the time when he came to accept it as the deepest desire of his heart.

In some ways the discernment of "fit" or "affinity" belongs more to intuition and common sense than to communicable rules. We cannot lay claim to the Spirit as if she were our reward for exertions of various types. What we need to do is continually ask of our spiritual life whether it resembles the generous outreach of love, the ability to "love first," that we know as one of the signs of grace.

The neglect of the experience of the Spirit in academic theology has on occasion been called "Christomonism" or "Jesusology." The former term is used most often by Orthodox theologians to describe the alleged Roman Catholic tendency to see everything in one-sided reference to Christ.[19] The Spirit, they say, then becomes merely an add-on, a means to carry out the already constituted ministries and sacraments of the church imaged as Body of Christ. The latter term, Jesusology, is used by Edward Schillebeeckx and others to call attention to a too literal dependence on the words and actions of Jesus of Nazareth, without taking appropriate account of the cosmic and mystical Christologies that appear to emerge naturally from a theology of the continued presence in another dimension of the risen Christ. A narrowing of God's action to what is mediated through the official interpretation of Christ's mission can be rightly criticized for leaving multiple aspects of human life today outside the light of grace. The Spirit becomes merely the energy by which the Word is sent. The goal of the Christian life becomes the imitation of Christ, no longer "deification" by the Holy Spirit. The charism is made subordinate to the institution, inner freedom to imposed authority, prophetism to juridicism, mysticism to scholasticism, the laity to the clergy, the universal priesthood to the ministerial hierarchy, and the college of bishops to the primacy of the pope. The Spirit, creative and renewing, cannot just be invoked to guard the institutional status quo. Madeleine L'Engle puts it this way: "To make community misunderstood is a powerful weapon of the Destroyer—to promise permanence, to insist on perfection, to strangle freedom, so that instead of having community we have a concentration camp."[20]

To be fair it should be noted that, while the Spirit was always interpreted as the assurer of infallibility for hierarchical structures, she was also seen as active in the inner lives of believers. This, however, is not an adequate pneumatology, if the division is so starkly between the private and the public, in effect subordinating the Spirit's action in the faithful to the public judgment of the institutional. The Pauline teaching that the Holy Spirit is present and active, through her gifts, in all believers gave way, as early as the third and fourth centuries, to an emphasis on the Spirit of unity requiring the submission of all to the same leader. Already in the writing of Ignatius of Antioch the analogy of One Body, One Head was succumbing to the literalization of an ideal (one God, one bishop, one faith). One wonders how much of this, along with the development of a certain kind of Christology in the West and deemphasis of the Spirit, had to do with the increasing claims of celibacy upon the leadership and the entrenchment of sex-negative theologies.

Christology in the perspective of the Spirit would enable Christians to better combine both the uniqueness and the universality of Jesus as Christ. It could show that there is no contradiction in disclosing the Spirit as operative in Christ in fullest measure and yet at work as the same Spirit in varying degrees everywhere in the history of the human race.

Sometimes God's work appears to be done directly by the Spirit without the mediation of institutional structure, and at other times through such mediation. The first is sometimes called the mystical principle and the second the sacramental principle. An example of mediacy would be Jesus' words, "He who receives you receives me . . . and him who sent me" (Matt. 10:40). An instance of immediacy in the New Testament is given in the story of the Holy Spirit who had already taken hold of Cornelius and his family before Peter came to baptize them (Acts 10:44–48). In both, it is the Spirit's work, giving life. This giving of life is not done only through the means instituted as continuous with the work of Christ. Neither church nor Bible can enclose the Spirit. God also intervenes directly in human lives, bringing the experience of liberation where it was not before and cannot be explained by the visible structures of secondary causality. Personal vitality sometimes resists the abstract rules that attempt to contain it, as Joan of Arc so well exemplifies. There are, as Congar puts it, "official and agreed positions—and there is reality."[21]

Now the Lord is the Spirit and where the Spirit of the Lord is, there is freedom (2 Cor. 3:17). In talk about sexuality, the weight of tradition has made it impossible for the conservers of the traditional forms to see how certain aspects of sexual life could be compatible with growth into the Spirit. This may be defensible in the framing of generalities, but not in particular judgments. The religious community is not only a traditional institution, it is a spiritual union of persons whose lives are directly responsive to the Spirit. The dynamic of the Spirit's presence is properly characterized as not "within them" but "between them." The church, moreover, is properly viewed as not the cause of the spread of the mystery through the world by the Holy Spirit, but rather as its *effect*, its result. As Walter Kasper formulates it, the "fellowship with God realized through the Spirit provides the foundation for the fellowship of the church."[22] Not metaphysically only, but existentially, in the order of encounter, the Spirit is first.

Such a view of the church would be characterized by a climate of freedom and trust, in which its vitality could bear fruit. The church is not just a closet for keeping past forms—a mothball ecclesiology—but without attention to a theology of the Holy Spirit it could become so. The future toward which the Spirit guides is uncertain; it is closer to Jesus' image of the householder who brings forth new things and old; it is to be viewed with hope, not suspicion. If we really believe that the Spirit of Jesus moves where she will, we cannot continue to use as criterion for discerning that Spirit only what we think we already know about Jesus from the Scriptures and the traditions of the churches. God's revelation and self-communication takes place as outpouring, walking as it were "without a net" in conditions of *kenosis* and the cross. There is no reverse in the symbolism of love to the death. St. Bernard says the Holy Spirit is the kiss which the Father and the Son give mutually to one another.[23] When we look to the images of the kiss and the outpouring of love to death we have gone about as far as we can go. The performance in real life of those images of God is obviously most profound in the context of sexual relation.

Contemporary efforts toward a theology of the Spirit see her action as disclosed in follower and leader alike. Rather than simply be the guarantor of the magisterium, the Spirit is understood to be responsible for the very tension between the sacralizing and the prophetic aspects of spirituality. This is the dynamic of God's creative motion: inner and outer, public and private, natural and supernatural, divine and human are no longer separate, locked spheres. Within this dynamic, the Spirit is the guarantee both of unity and diversity. Unity is sought, not in submission to the authority of a single leader, but in "reciprocal relationships and in consensus."[24]

The effect on ecclesiology of a more fully developed theology of the Spirit is not hard to imagine. The effect on the everyday lives of believers, used to shunting whole areas of their lives into the artificially constructed categories of the secular and the profane, would be wholly transformed if they could see the Spirit as its integrating power. This work of re-creation and reconciliation could be imaged as the weaving of a seamless robe from the unraveled strands that ages of wrong choices, ignorance, and forced subordination of the weaker by the more powerful continue to produce. People enter into union with that work, not only in the *epiclesis* of the eucharist and ordination, but also in invoking the Spirit in the *epiclesis* which is the human sexual kiss and offer of unconditional self-gift. The "calling forth" of the Holy Spirit emphasizes that only in and by the Spirit of God does the church live and act. As has been pointed out, it may be possible to say where the church is, where faith, vitality, hospitality, justice, love are, but not possible to say where it is not. We simply do not know the outer boundaries of the Spirit's activity in the world, nor do we dare to claim we know all of the ways in which she acts. We develop theories of discernment, but they are our theories and have not been "endorsed" by a divine hermeneutic. Even where the church in official statements of consensus, speaks to the issue, its language is suggestive of the expectation of a wider interpretation, one that takes into account the local and the temporal. The Spirit is active in the religious needs felt by people, says the Constitution on the Church in the Modern World. Every movement toward justice and every "putting aside of love of self" can be attributed to the activity of the Spirit.[25] By that criterion, nowhere has the Spirit been more active during the past two thousand years than in the sexuality of women. The linking of sexuality with Holy Spirit rather than original sin begins a new chapter in the history of theology. "From the beginning until now the entire creation, as we know, has been groaning in one great act of giving birth; and not only creation, but all of us who possess the first fruits of the Spirit, we too groan inwardly as we wait for our bodies to be set free." And "I am certain of this: neither death nor life, no angel, no prince, nothing that exists, nothing still to come, not any power, or height or depth, nor any created thing can ever come between us and the love of God made visible in Christ Jesus our Lord" (Rom. 8:22, 38).

What is the truth that is to be discerned about human sexuality? How does this truth come to light? The truth of Scripture is of God's fidelity and God's plan of grace, not any one generation's interpretation of what that plan includes or excludes. The range of God's fidelity is continually being revealed as it is carried out in time by the Spirit. This truth has to do with our destinies, that is, it is eschatological, not metaphysical, for the sake of our salvation, addressed to the heart which is called to do the truth. It always has a psychological and moral character for human beings.

But another theme, that of the Spirit as cosmic creator, is also finding new development in a time of concern for the health of the planet and of renewed consciousness of being members of a cosmic community. At this time, near the millennial turning point, when our vision of the universe is immensely greater and more dynamic in its development than what Paul apparently meant by "creation," that is, all beings who are not God, we are also aware of a greater degree of immersion in nature. We know that we participate in the earth, reflectively, but as part of an ecosystem, not above it. An eleven-year-old girl, interviewed on Earth Day, said, apparently quite unaware of her theological insight: "we are not like your generation, thinking you are above everything; we know we are part of the earth and depend on it."

As immanent Spirit, God creates everything in the world that is constantly "new and fresh, free and vital, unexpected and mighty, at once tender and strong." As the Spirit of grace, God's self-communication to the outside is known as the interior call, and the "secret power of transformation within us." The process of re-creation toward which the universe and humankind is involved is a process of liberation. That is one of the fruits by which the Spirit is known. Wherever human beings refuse to conform to legalism and mediocrity, the Spirit is at work. The desire for freedom is no longer a sporadic gift, but appears to have been given to the world as a prophetic task. Teilhard de Chardin wrote in *The Divine Milieu*[26] about the kind of spirituality he saw as revealing itself in people of our time: it showed itself in a dedication to the tasks of human progress. It was ultimately a "mysticism of co-creative union," involving an awareness of the two hands of God, one that is merged in us with the sources of life, and the other "whose embrace is so wide that, at slightest pressure, all the springs of the universe respond harmoniously together." He saw a twofold pattern in our development as well: one essential element being what we do through the call of our own energy; the other being the forces of diminishment that gives us opportunity to grow by what we undergo. He wrote: "That Christ may enter deeply into us, we need alternately the work that dilates the heart and the sorrow that brings death to it, the life that enlarges a man in order that he may be sanctifiable and the death that diminishes him in order that he may be sanctified."[27]

When a person's mind is opened to the Spirit, the first thing he knows is that he is a sinner. The awareness of sin, primarily one's own sin (that we are not above everything), is the first insight given by God's Spirit of wisdom. But to the extent that human beings reject their destiny as secondary causes, refusing to carry out that work of renewal of which the Spirit is the agent, the earth too suffers in continued abuse. Women and men sharing responsibility for reproductive capacity, finding in the spiritual dimensions of their sexual attraction the motive to act upon it or not, is an example of the "first fruits" of a responsible attitude toward the whole of creation. Sexuality is of God not just as the procreative capacity by which God the creator is imitated; it is also God's as the liberating and fulfilling mode of co-creation by which the Spirit sustains the universe.

Sexual partnership then is not only the great mystery which shows something of the relationship between Christ and church; its sacramental function also extends to the cosmic partnership between Spirit and universe. This is an image that no longer implies subordination. Because it assumes equality and mutuality, because it emphasizes immanence more than transcendence, it is more appropriate to our time and speaks prophetically to our relationships to each other as well as to our solidarity with the earth.

To say this with some enthusiasm is not to affirm what would be patently ridiculous: that there are no forces of diminishment or evil. It is rather to say that the Spirit of God is prior and partner to people in their struggle toward liberation from self-destruction, self-hatred, and hatred of the Spirit. Thus to have the Spirit of God is not to be sinless, for that is not fully possible. It is rather to know what sin is, to know one's own sins and the sins of the world, and to acknowledge them with genuine humility and repentance. This is the paradox of the spiritual life: to know one's sins and to confess them is to be liberated from them, for it is to know that sins are remembered no more in the final messianic covenant (Jer. 31:34). Once sin is seen for what it is, continually and perpetually acknowledged by the grace of God's Spirit within, the way is clear for genuine human growth and development. Here, however, it is important to remember the lesson of the parables: what look like weeds in the wheat may not be such; do not be too ready to act on your first impressions of what constitutes evil, for it may be merely the messiness of creation.

Fear blocks the creativity of the Spirit. But not all fear is psychological refusal to love or trust. There are also the innate fears that are associated with being a body with a specific structure. The female's structure leaves her open to fear of forced entry, of sexual violation based on superior strength or economic usefulness. Courage is the virtue which acts toward love in the face of fear. Being the gatekeeper, the one who opens herself to being entered, even when willingly, by penetration, what may feel like invasion, is a position requiring wisdom. (Wisdom is prudence plus courage.) Ultimately procreation requires the overcoming of this physical fear in a woman, but in itself procreation does not offer effective motivation; desire allows her to open her body for sexual entry. A male biological basis for fear exists as well. It is the fear of loss of autonomy, of connection, of being reabsorbed, not just physically but psychologically, into the world of women from which his whole gender identity has forced him to separate. He must trust entering, and having done so, trust exiting. Fear and courage, prudence and wisdom—these are the comings and goings of Spirit active in personal sexual life.

Life passages as paschal mystery

A spiritual guide, trained in the tradition of Hatha Yoga, was asked: "How can we recognize when there is an opportunity for growth? Surely if we knew about it, we would seize it, whatever it would take." His answer disappointed some because it took away the hope for a specialized mysticism and restored the discussion to real life. He answered: "Wherever there is anxiety and guilt, whenever there is depression, sorrow, and loss, wherever a person is taken by surprise, there is opportunity for growth." It is like the question asked of Jesus, "Good Master, what must I do to gain salvation?" (Mark 10:17), and his answer, which definitely took the questioner by surprise, as he began to recite the well-known commandments of the covenant and the social use of the most material element of all, money. Then he turned toward Jerusalem and shared with them what he was to undergo: condemnation by the system of justice he honored, betrayal, ridicule, death. And that he was to come through. Moreover, "the cup I shall drink, you shall drink" (Mark 10:39). Nothing extraordinary: loss, depression, anxiety, guilt, sorrow; the stuff of adult life. And in the midst of it—taken by surprise by God.

How explicit does the inserting of sexual experience into the spiritual journey have to be? Not explicit at all at the level of physical action. The reality is that we are in Christ, in God, in the Spirit. Reflective thought strains and agonizes to stuff that reality into words, but never entirely successfully. Even years later, in events that break through the routine of things, particularly adequate words can flash back to people the truth that always was theirs. That truth is not about Jesus or other holy people, back then. It's about us, now. What the retelling of the paschal mystery does is to provide a long-running series in which one's own episode makes sense. It tells us that life is a spiritual journey which includes the experience of sin, though not always one's own. It documents the response to a call and the experience of the passion, which cannot be escaped if one is not to refuse finally to undergo the claims of vocation. The paschal mystery is known also in the experience, not just once, and certainly not just after death, of "coming through," of having been delivered from the place we thought we were buried for good.

Accepting the paschal mystery as one's own story breaks down the sin (inside or outside oneself) through which human beings become curved in upon themselves. Even as an image, the series of narrow passages through which one comes out into the light emphasizes the "ecstatic" character of the Spirit. She opens things which are crusted shut and brings them to fulfillment. Addictions are the opposite of ecstasy; they are effective symbols among us of sin as closed eyes and clenched fists, shrinking from reality. Through them we act out being closed around things smaller than us. To enter into the paschal mystery is a way to recover wholeness and human freedom. In no way does this resemble what is usually meant by the term "perfection." With characteristic wisdom, Teilhard wrote:

Right to the end we shall carry with us a burden of inconsistencies and
unachieved aims: the great thing is to have found the center of unification, God, and to have tried loyally throughout our lives to make him
reign in our own person—the little fragment of being that we rule and
that is so little our own.[28]

Ultimately life means being open to death, which is itself the fundamental
ecstasy. The longing of the human heart is for a communion even beyond
death. This is the restlessness, the longing, the desire for God that is practiced
in the parable of sexual partnership.

More than through the family meal, Christians will understand what the
eucharist is saying about communion when they can think of sexual sharing of
body in a sacred mode. This is the missing pre-evangelization, not unrelated to
eating, but together with eating, symbolic of the deepest communion to which
they both point—communion with God. One might even hypothesize and say
that, far from being inappropriate before communion, sex ought to be required
before communion. Put another way, ritual communion might well be delayed
until its meaning through sexual union can be known experientially. The
conjunction would protect both against trivialization; their meanings belong
together like shape and shadow.

What you have when you do this,
is a moment of grace.
What began as lunch,
can end as eucharist
or reconciliation
or healing
or whatever you call it.[29]

THEOLOGY OF MORALITY

Sins must be spoken of openly when one is serious about sexual-spiritual
integration. I reject the view that sex always collapses into sin when elaborate
safeguards are not in place. Yet, when my students object to the statement that
we are all sinners, because they hear that we are nothing but sin, they are
victims of that same fallacy. They affirm from their own experience, however,
that they have all done things of which they are ashamed. I think the latter
formulation is acceptable to them because it distinguishes the actions from the
core of the person. Too many people have known the destructiveness and pain of
sex to believe a version of it that fails to recognize that it carries potential for

the experience of sin. The adult who has awakened to her own sexual vocation should be far beyond the understanding of sin as material transgression of taboos. Understandings of sin that correlate more adequately to adult moral development stress inner choice as well as the habitual character of the behavior. As an "option" rather than a single act, it is characterized by moral significance and depth of consent. Spiritual directors have a rule of thumb: nothing done just once is either truly good or truly evil.

The norm for virtue is not necessarily the law. The norm is human authenticity—to be all that we are created to be. "The created self," says William Huebsch, "is a self-for-others, self-with-earth, self-open-unto-mystery."[30] To be called sin, a pattern of behavior is assumed to be present which deliberately betrays the core of that vocation. Huebsch has a particularly provocative notion of sin as the "failure to pause":

> *The failure to pause will drive us away from*
> *ourselves,*
> *it will prevent us from being authentic,*
> *and therefore, it is sinful.*
> *I think this is among the most serious sins*
> *it is possible for us to commit.*
> *It is much more serious than*
> *the traditional "bad" sins:*
> *those against purity.*[31]

It is important to acknowledge that as we have multiple models of God so we have models of sin. To pretend to a single adequate definition of sin would be naive or arrogant. Evelyn Underhill, discussing sin and grace, identifies a pattern by which the spiritual life struggles to emerge among us. She says that the essence of much sin is conservatism: "It is rooted in the tendency of the instinctive life to go on, in changed circumstances, acting in the same old way."[32] Correspondingly, virtue is rightness of correspondence with our present surroundings, and consistency of our deeds with our best ideas. This is what I have referred to repeatedly as authenticity. The asceticism of authenticity is in dealing with change. While the myth could be sustained that sexuality belonged to nature, then the mark of virtue might have been to go on acting in the same perennial ways, and sin would have been associated with innovation and adjustment to the contemporary scene. This view of asceticism as change forces us to use on new and higher levels the strategies of habit formation which have been so successful in transforming the human race through scientific and political modes of operation. Taboos that would control sexual life within old and established channels then become clearly more of the problem than of the solution. "Many of our vices, in fact, are simply savage qualities—and some are even savage virtues—in their old age." "When qualities which were once useful on their own level are outgrown . . . and check the movement towards life's spiritualization, then—whatever they may be—they belong to the body of death, not to the body of life, and are 'sin.' "[33]

Capitulation to sin is often brought about by mere sloth, which Julian of Norwich declares to be one of the two most deadly sicknesses of the soul. Sometimes yielding to a starved and repressed side of one's nature (violence, sexual passion) is like giving in to an old and primitive craving, which religious or social morality has temporarily kept in check. To deny too violently such natural instincts is to court their revenge. This view of sin, as primarily a retreat to past levels of conduct and experience, a defeat of the spirit of the future in its conflict with the undefeated past, gives a fresh view of what humanity needs to be freed from in its journey to sexual wholeness. It suggests that the way of integration is to harness the "fiery energies and impulses to the light."[34] In psychological terminology it would seek the healing of conflict through the unification of instinctive life and rational life. "The wrong way to do it," continues Underhill, "is seen in the methods of the Puritan and extreme ascetic where all animal impulse is regarded as 'sin' and repressed, a proceeding which involves the risk of grave physical and mental disorder, and produces even at the best a bloodless pietism."[35] That bloodless pietism is what many still expect when they hear the term spirituality. The ordering of love rightly according to our present surroundings and consistency between our actions and our best ideas is then the task that confronts the person who wants to contribute to the making of our sexual morality.

A third model of sin that has been useful to some in their spiritual growth, especially from overly individualistic and self-centered moralistic forms, is sin as "contempt for the vulnerable."[36] This image is biblical and it is particularly applicable to sexuality for it challenges the self-hatred and body rejection which for some still passes as spirituality. In sexuality our vulnerability is particularly marked. Contempt for it is sin; pretensions toward total self-sufficiency and self-control are sin.

The interesting thing about morality is that while there are so many and different moral systems, the need of persons who live by them is to find justification for a way of life that is not just one among many. Intellectually, the many human ways of responding to life situations and conflicts can be seen as comparable, but in the practical order the human being often has to feel she lives by morality itself, the one and only right way. It is never a pleasant experience when a person begins to realize that not only might she have a problem living according to the morality she has considered obvious and certain, but that this morality is in conflict with another—with similar claims to certitude—either within or outside her community. When such an event takes place it is more than one's "sinlessness" that is at stake; it is the authority and credibility of the community. In sexual issues, moral innovation and diversity are particularly unwelcome, for sexual taboos in some ways define community cohesiveness. Breaking these taboos or, even more, "shedding" them deliberately establishes a person effectively as an outsider, an "excommunicate" in the original sense of that term. Insofar as a rule is not internalized and personally appropriated, it generally leads either to a passive and inauthentic conformity, or to rebellion and conflict. The challenge is that the norms should be useful as guidelines for living, without becoming some sort of ready-made straitjacket, imposed on people to curtail their legitimate life.

But loss of the certitude of childhood is, as we have seen, a stage in the growth process. The person then is issued an invitation to moral adulthood. In order to act he must work out the grounds for his own conduct, and for the first time he uses moral reasoning as a skill ordered to practical decision-making. He does not need to formulate just an acceptable way to act in a single situation; he needs to relate this reason for this action to "the human way to be," in the universal sense that was suggested in our discussion of vocation. An action must fit her vocation, not just her lifestyle; her membership in humankind, not just her unique needs. In the most general sense, no act can be good which does not issue from a free person choosing freely, nor which infringes in some way on the essential right of other persons freely to fulfil themselves, nor which fails to respect the nonhuman world of animals and plants as themselves teleological centers.

Yet to expect to find some specific moral norms that are universally applicable would be mistaken. Actual morality is in persons, and persons are particular, not universal. Every moral system, while open to the universal and transcendent, is historical and contingent. A rule—such as the prohibition of forced or deceptive sexual encounter—emerges, in accordance with social and historical change, out of a concern for just relations between the sexes. It would not always have been apparent that this was a necessary way of acknowledging the humanity of women. At one time the rule would have required women to be accessible to any male who desired her. Acknowledging the right of refusal and consent to both men and women makes both human, as this is understood in our world. Therefore it is appropriate as a particular rule or guideline for action. Forced conformity to an outdated imperative, precisely one which is no longer connected to the humanness of the moral subject, does violence; it is destructive to a conscience because it no longer transmits the moral energy or spiritual growth of which it should be the vehicle.

Historical research has shown that the institutionalization of marriage and the severely restrictive rules for sexual behavior, often put forward as Christian norms and as based on natural law, are in fact the norms that developed in bourgeois society that arose between the sixteenth and nineteenth centuries. They were in close affinity with the churches because of patriarchal influences, and this is why the churches put forth such extraordinary effort to spread them. Unfortunately, universal validity has been claimed for those norms.

The New Testament, also, contains parenesis, that is, "exhortations," which often take the form of the repetition of received teaching, not new moral reasoning. The fundamental reason for acting morally is presented as new—to be in Christ—but the assumption is that the older catalogues of what is or is not sinful can be simply taken over without rethinking. The particular Pauline parenesis in 1 Corinthians, for example, is of historical, not normative, significance.[37] It is a "remake" of an old film, not a revision responding to new realities. Paul makes it clear that he is not giving directives out of a special revelation, but presupposing what everyone knows and agrees on. We always have the challenge of figuring out precisely what is being condemned or warned against in an ancient, translated text. For example, *porneia* (usually translated "fornication") in 1 Corinthians 6 is still argued about, with at least three interpretations contending for acceptance: it could mean (a) sex as used for religious worship, called idolatrous because it followed the custom of the pagan cults; (b) stable but irregular relationships; (c) *all* irregular relationships (which of course begs the question of what should be considered irregular relationships). Another example occurs in 1 Corinthians 9 where the *malakoi* (*molles*) are said to be excluded from the kingdom of God. For centuries this text was understood to mean the rejection of masturbation; today we are informed that this is a faulty translation. The moral theologian Joseph Fuchs points out that not even the Vatican declaration on sexual ethics (1975) invokes this text any longer as an argument against masturbation. The point of the examples is to affirm that our Scriptures cannot provide an excuse for abandoning the responsibility to continue reasoning about moral issues; they do not contain prerecorded answers to contemporary questions.

Accepting the task of rethinking what it is to act humanly is equivalent to discovering a fundamental option. It could be seen as somewhat equivalent to the notion of directing one's heart toward good or evil. Thoughts and actions arising from our sexual potential are morally significant, though neither more nor less so than other actions that call upon the "whole" of an adult, that proceed from her center of acts. It has been an anomaly in the Christian moral tradition that single actions of a sexual nature were presumed, without consideration for knowledge, consent, or circumstances, to represent a moral "option." Thus they were judged to be either blameless (as within marriage) or mortally sinful (as in any circumstances other than legal, heterosexual marriage). The presupposition follows from at least two mistakes: that coitus is denoted as the explicit goal and intentionality of all sexual feelings and actions, and that there is no possibility of a lesser or greater moral significance in the area of sexuality, that is, that there are in effect no "single acts" in sexual life. The effect on individuals, especially women who internalized this perception, was that there could be no mistakes in the arena of sexual relation. It was, contrary to explicit biblical teaching, the "unforgivable sin" in many women's consciousness. This becomes a fact with tragic consequences where it is realized that few choose clearly their sexual life; most acquiesce to what family, society, or partners chose for them. As the most dangerous area morally, it was also the one least one's own to control. No wonder the questions of sexual morality, when not irrelevant textbook exercises, looked more like taboos than principles to guide a holy and happy life. Until the fairly recent past, wrote Yves Congar, there was, it seemed, only one virtue—obedience, and only one sin—that of the 'flesh.'[38] No wonder the rules were enforced with sanctions, maintained with restrictions, and surrounded with religious fear rather than examined, evaluated, and appropriated through education.

A major turning point in the history of sexual morality occurred when Augustine's theory, that original sin was transmitted by the act of copulation, was accepted as doctrine. This extreme version of one (but not the only) theology of original sin, when taken as the basis for moral teaching has tended to appeal to those who, for whatever reason, are pessimistic about human motives and the human capacity for responsible action. So it has played into the hands of the pornographers and the rapists as well as those who want all sexual expression carefully governed within a patriarchal marriage. The hope for moral transformation has no place in their sexual arena. By contrast, recent Roman Catholic teachings regarding politics and economics counts precisely on the human capacity for self-regulation. They envision the possibility of a just and peaceful society and call for voluntary action to make that hope a reality. The political agenda follows from optimism regarding virtue over concupiscence. Again by contrast, the agenda currently reflecting sexual assumptions—especially that on abortion—invokes public condemnation, fear, and legal sanctions, thus revealing its basic pessimism.

So the tragedy is one of omission: for want of a theology of sexuality based on baptismal identity and responsibility, a morality of responsibility regarding sexual issues was left undeveloped. We cannot enter upon an authentic relationship to our sexuality without theological meaning that grounds an ethics. Because sexual self-expression is concerned with relations with others, it has ethical consequences.

For the same reason, that sexuality performs our connectedness, the ethical formulation must provide for the participation of the community in providing a forum for both raising and resolving its ambiguity. Mere repetitive exhortation is no longer adequate. Authenticity requires adaptation to change. In the dialectic whereby decision-making is not just a one-way application of the norm, the community itself can be renewed in the effort to refine a sexual ethic that promotes spiritual growth.

Adult moral decision-making is integral to adult spirituality, not just as individuation but in the service of community renewal. This is also why morality needs spirituality. As life needs rules, so rules need to be stretched regularly to respond to life. Some regular method needs to be adopted and trusted, so that human forethought and planning are valued within the sexual arena as in other adult decisions.

The current moral theology about sexual expression is showing that some change has come out of listening to the stories of those who express their love sexually. Attempts to distinguish signs of sin from signs of grace show evidence of inductive reasoning and reflection on practice. No longer is it considered appropriate to impose on this experience a model which was created without reference to it and is managed from outside it. For the first time, in the Pastoral Constitution on the Church in the Modern World, marriage is recognized as *in its sexuality* the singular expression and completion of the spouses' love, their primary way of performing their intention for total self-gift. Earlier documents would have found in the sexual impulse an inescapably selfish concupiscence asserting itself. But the tension between the magisterium's ameliorating judgment on sex and the simultaneous tenacity of the ancient bias against sexual expression continues to appear within official and unofficial theological materials.

Within those foundational comments, what I propose is the following set of steps for practical sexual decision-making.

1. Be clear on who you are and what you choose to become. This is the basis of all morality. The indicative precedes the imperative. A person starts where she is, with her self-knowledge, her commitments and sense of vocation. Integrity is to choose action continuous with one's dynamic center.

2. Consult all the sources of wisdom which are available to you. Sources of moral reasoning include Scripture, tradition, communal and personal experience, law, imagination and works of the imagination, moral rules, family of origin with customs and cultural values. Imagine all these as consultants around a table. They do not all have the same deliberative vote, but are assigned priority according to your unique situation and history. All should, however, be attended to.

3. Ask: What are the alternatives to the action presenting itself? If a person thinks she has no alternatives, she is too isolated, too dependent, or has stopped thinking too soon. Then assistance should be sought before proceeding. Action without alternatives is not free, and therefore not a moral choice. It

is of course also possible to sabotage one's own moral agency by deliberately putting oneself in a situation of reduced freedom, for example, by intoxication. This is culpable to the extent that one is aware of it and consents to it. It is always to settle for less than the personal and spiritual adulthood one is destined for. It may be helpful to think in terms of two steps in the deliberate choice of a wrong action, that is, (a) deliberate self-deception and (b) acting on the self-deception.

4. What are the consequences for the primary participants? for their wider network of relationships? for society as a whole. Usually the consequences are not between good and evil but between variations or degrees of the good. Moreover, one is aware that the long-term consequences of an action are not always immediately visible and the short-term consequences may be overturned. Here one's "hierarchy of values" becomes pertinent.

5. What choice, given the self-understanding, data, and evaluation of consequences, will I make? A choice is not a further step beyond reasoning; it is choosing to stop the reasoning process by the intervention of the will in order to get on with what life requires, that is, action. The alternative to making an imperfect choice is worse: it is not to act at all, which is in effect never to become a moral agent, a fully functioning spiritual person.

6. Am I at peace with this decision? To act out of an unresolved doubt or a troubled conscience is destructive to the person. One can identify a right choice in advance of the action by the peace of mind and soul the decision brings, and a wrong choice by the guilt it initiates. One should of course be sure by consulting of sources (step 2 above) that one is not acting out of false conscience, scrupulosity, or unhealthy guilt. Anxiety (What would my mother say?) or bravado (I wish X could see me now!) might indicate such unreadiness to take this action because it shows a morbid excitement rather than a sense of legitimate pleasure in expressing one's deepest self. The importance of a well-formed conscience is obvious. It is the result of education and a habit of right choices. It is more like a developed skill, such as aesthetic taste, than an infused gift. Though one should never act in bad faith, there comes a time when the moral calculus must end, and one can act, in good faith, though not always with complete certainty. Then faith provides the certainty that even when wrong choices are made in good faith, the person's spirituality is not diminished but can grow. God's forgiveness never fails. As Julian of Norwich wrote, "There is no wrath in God." When people have difficulty believing in the forgiveness of God and others, it may well be because they have not yet been able to forgive themselves. This takes us back to step 1: What do I wish to become?

Erotic feeling alone does not make sex moral. Sexual acts and desires have their own reality and value; piggy-backing on the absolute value of erotic feeling is neither necessary nor helpful. Structures of justice, development, reconciliation are all part of the spiritual life. The virtues of courage, prudence, wisdom are all important. When mere obedience is replaced by mere emotion, spiritual adulthood, nuanced as virtue responsive to reality, is still distant. Eros itself piggy-backs on the appropriate choice of value.

FOCAL POINTS:

It is not enough to say that it should become possible to put God in sex; the point is that it is impossible to have authentic sex except in God.

The Holy Spirit carries on God's transformative action in the ordinary events of everyday life. The Spirit is experienced, not precisely as Spirit, but as forgiveness, hope, desire for transcendence, acceptance of vulnerability.

Moral decision-making is a skill that can be learned.

6

Being and Doing

If a way to the better there be, it exacts a full look at the worst.
Rainer Maria Rilke, *Duino Elegies* 9

We, let it be once more insisted, We are these transformers of the earth, our whole existence, the flights and plunges of our love, all fit us for this task (in comparison with which there is, essentially no other).
Rainer Maria Rilke, *Letters from Muzot*

Chapter 5 indicated the importance of life-talk for God-talk. This one asserts the second half of the same truth. Life-talk that produces people with great hearts and great capacities to love assumes an openness to a dimension beyond the empirical. Since spiritually active human beings are made, not born, it is appropriate to reflect on characteristics and experiences that advance such formation. Being, more than doing, is the traditional concern of spiritual growth counselors, but that quality of being invariably manifests itself in action, including mentoring, ministering, and friendship.

FORMATION

The ability to relate, to enter into long-term contact with another person, to be open, to become a friend involves skills that can be learned, but comes in terms of its motivation from a different, deeper source. It flows from values that are so integrated in the self that they may not even be known objectively. Eroticism that is spiritual but not disembodied, that reaches out in openness, this is the standard by which sexual health can ultimately be judged. Progress toward that goal, an eroticism consonant with spiritual growth, an attitude of making love that graces the world, can be learned. Two disclaimers are necessary here. No complete program for such education exists; if a curriculum were to be drawn up, it would have to encompass more of life than is presently accepted as the sphere of church or school. At the same time, while growing up is obviously a social process to which many factors contribute, there is already too much debate about whose responsibility it is to control sex education and too little about what kind of person is envisioned. Progress toward wholeness in sexual-spiritual subjects will never be made, comparable to that which centuries of deliberate and systematic emphasis on training the intellect has produced, so long as more effort is spent on preventing the discussion than on imagining its possibilities.

For many the vision of a spiritual journey was lacking during the first stages of their sexual awakenings. Many eventually set out on a remedial quest for spiritual growth, one that they desire explicitly to include sexual development. Just as the first initiation into sexual adulthood was taken, not alone, but with others, so this "second" time through is not just a personal but a communal journey. When the adult personal life yields the realization that all models somehow have failed it, yet the journey of growth must continue, then one is ready for the insight that comes out of the Christian theology of initiation. The precise meaning of being adult is to have no human model, but to find one's way, as a physical copy but a spiritual original, to make the divine model present in a new way. The acceptance of oneself as adult, on a spiritual journey, includes the acceptance of a way that is not exactly like anyone else's, but finds its uniqueness in living out a particular identification with the Christ. The way to sexual-spiritual wholeness is within the community, but it is not so much of the community or the community's wisdom as it is of the Spirit who speaks to each heart. Those "words" are spoken out again as individual lives which "fill up what is lacking" in our experience of God through Christ. Through confident self-acceptance as beings with a sexual-spiritual task, we proclaim the hard truths, the human-divine Christ, the God of *kenosis* poured out in multiple symbols of love. The challenge of this chapter is to exemplify, through brief reflection on practical aspects of friendship and of ministry that spiritual growth is both social and personal, both gift and task.

To make spiritual-sexual integration an aspect of all forms of being and doing requires the establishment of what Kenneth Leech calls an "ecology of the spirit."[1] It consists of illumination, that is, "enlightening the eyes of the heart" (Eph. 1:18), with a new vision of how the sexual and spiritual interrelate, as well as new skills and functions. To the imagery of vision and light I prefer that of warmth and desire. To "fan the flame of the heart's desire" with the new energy of a hunger that may hope to be fulfilled also liberates new motivations and ministries. "Skill in the service of value" is one way that virtue has been defined. It may be time to re-energize the virtue of chastity by associating it with the methods successful in advancing sexual and spiritual growth. Those who thought it was enough to tell people that they were not to be greedy, lustful, or selfish have discovered that it is not enough to exercise the contrary virtues when these have less prestige than the alternatives of conspicuous consumption, exploitation of others, and narcissistic self-absorption. More is required: a positive commitment to spiritual growth that engages with the world. As Simone Weil wrote, "Whoever is only incapable of being as brutal, violent and inhuman as the adversary, yet without exercising the opposite virtues, is inferior to this adversary in both inner strength and prestige; and they will not hold their own against them."[2] She was, of course, speaking of the inadequacy of simple nonviolence as a counter to violence. Only disciplined and organized love is strong enough. The same point holds here. The societal attempt to reject sexual violence, disease, ignorance, promiscuity, and exploitation are doomed to failure until the strong opposite virtues—the virtues of integrated sexual-spiritual love—are exercised in a constant and effective manner.

Spirituality delivers an experience of depth and largeness in life. Whether or not an individual names that depth and height as God, its source remains the same. When spiritual hunger is felt, people often reach out, seeking to change things that have revealed themselves to be of spiritual importance because their lives have become narrow, limited, and closed in upon themselves. Those who as professionals help others to change their lives give the following steps as proved successful. The pattern coincides with the classic disciplines for spiritual growth.

1. Self-knowledge: Examine your life to see how the behavior you want to change began, what triggers it, what the hidden rewards are that make it so hard to change. Some recommend keeping a diary for at least two weeks to help pinpoint these details (is it tension, anger, loneliness, fatigue, the friends or others who lure you into the behavior?). "I meditated twice a day and basically asked two questions" wrote one woman. "What do you want me to do? How do I need to change?"

2. A definite plan: Set a date for quitting or beginning. Establish intermediate goals and rewards.

3. An altered environment: Avoid the places or persons that encourage the behavior; remove the sources of temptation.

4. Alternatives: Find healthy replacements for things or actions you want to renounce. It is important to fill the space with alternative pleasures or activities. Exercise, service to others with similar problems, prayer—all are ways of filling the void that's left.

5. Renaming: Think of yourself differently. See yourself as one who now

controls her temper or makes time for spiritual reflection. The imaging of a new identity protects a person from falling back into those actions that do not fit.

6. Community: Ask for support. Enlist the help of family, friends, and co-workers. Tell them you want and need their help.

7. Prayer: Praying is one of the oldest and best methods of healing for human beings. It is not even necessary to know or name to whom the prayer is directed. The prayer itself is a response to an initiative perhaps dimly felt, from a source larger than, and other than, the self.

8. Forgiveness: Plan a strategy. It is important to cope with the inevitable failure, so that it does not become a major fall. The strength of an old pattern makes it normal that one should fall back into it. A strategy for relapse does not mean you are now a permanent failure and need not try any longer. Learn what happened and why, so that perhaps next time it can be avoided. Compulsions or addictions differ from habits, which are simply ways of behaving that have become ingrained by repetition. When something has become compulsive it is not simply automatic because it has been done so often as to become habitual. It is automatic because it is obeying unconscious motives. With addictions there is a loss of freedom. The person realizes more and more that she has fallen under their control. Compulsions, since they are more difficult to change than habits, may require professional advice or the joining of a recovery program. Then spiritual growth becomes possible as part of the "aftercare," in the language of the therapist.

SELF-WORTH AND BODY IMAGE

One of the key factors to developing a relatively untroubled sexual life is a strong sense of self-worth. Everyone has feelings and ideas about self; positive or negative, these are expressed in behavior. As the ability to value one's self and to treat oneself with dignity and respect, self-esteem can vary not just in terms of quality, that is, negative or positive, but also in degree; and it can rise or fall in response to everyday experiences. When a person's sense of self-worth is high, everything seems to flow unchecked: change is possible, love is trusted, challenges are welcome. Secure in his own self-worth, he is able to ask for help, yet knows he is his own best resource. He can accept all his feelings, without having to act on every one of them. Intelligence directs actions; she knows she can choose. Decisions are made without undue concern.

Vitality is associated with a high degree of self-esteem. This should be distinguished from what is sometimes called "flying high" where a person is the last to realize that she is overextended. Nor is it the same as what is referred to as being "full of oneself," wherein a person's self-absorption cushions him from awareness of limitations that are easily perceived by others. While common experience reveals that particular times of fatigue or crisis can temporarily lessen feelings of self-worth, it also indicates that this is temporary. The person with higher self-esteem can acknowledge negative feelings because she knows they are not her ultimate truth. The person with low self-esteem is more likely to deny or repress them. Not the ebb and flow, but the steady level of one's sense of self has more to do with what happens both in her inner life and her relational life than any other factor.

A feeling of little worth opens the door to a person becoming a victim. In sexual matters this has significant and long term consequences. To defend the vulnerable self, one may hide behind walls of distrust and isolation or even strike out at others in fear. Fear is one form that evil takes. It first blinds us, keeping us from taking risks and thereby finding new ways to solve problems. The fear can be disarmed by dealing with present problems, one at a time, formulated in manageable units. By contrast, when there is a sense of global unsolved and unsolvable problems, helplessness thrives. Often the next step is to label oneself as a failure or loser, and since it is necessary to escape from these painful feelings, one becomes vulnerable to drugs, alcohol, overeating, or self-alienating sexual behavior. The spiritual sense that failure and loss is an aspect of the human condition—its finitude and its potential—is very different from the tendency to personalize and identify fully with every inadequacy. An appropriate sense of fallibility in fact is a countering influence to the need to be perfect, and the tendency to fall into despair at the realization of one's own imperfection. A balance must be struck in our spiritual education between the conviction that we are common (the same as others, with common limitations of humanity) and that we are unique (the fullest actualization of our particular gifts). Either overdeveloped without the other puts people at risk of expecting too much or too little of themselves. Either way, they fail the test they give themselves. As an individual comes to understand her own heart, she can identify which aspect is in need of reinforcement and pay herself the respect of seeing to it. (This is the situation Isabel is in at the end of *Final Payments*, when she thinks she has been too proud and selfish and therefore tries to humiliate herself. But in fact she comes to see that she is suffering from self-hate because she has not been able to forgive herself for being physical.) The spiritual discipline that helps one cope with negative feelings of self-worth is a two-step process. It involves articulating the negative feelings, so they can be made objective and assessed. To devalue one's feelings is to devalue oneself. Admitting these feelings, one can build for oneself the sense of being able to cope, on another occasion, with the situation that caused them. One can in fact change: explicitly choose to change the way he responded to the situation that produced such negative feelings. One man wrote about his sense of anger and despair when finding the words "Death to gays" written on a bathroom wall. A period of high-risk behavior followed, which he understood, upon reflection, to be a way of acting out his internalization of that public message: he was supposed to be dead. The beginning of healing for him was to be able to say, "I deserve to live. I have a right to live."

The second step involves turning within to hear the word of love spoken unceasingly in one's very existence. A simple phrase like "I have been loved enough . . ." can produce the assurance that builds confidence. One copes with imperfection, even injustice, not by swallowing it, repressing it, denying it, or identifying with it, but by putting it in context. "You take the fear out and replace it with love." My vocation is to become human in my way with my particular characteristics. My breathing, seeing, smelling, my existence is a message of love and hope from the Spirit, whom I love in loving my own spirit. In self-talk, a form of pre-prayer, I can change the feeling from one of false self-hatred to one of hope. Faith enables me to love first, because I know I have been loved enough. The self-hater is the name of the tempter; Christ named self-love as the standard for neighbor-love.

Healthy levels of self-worth grow more reliably in an atmosphere that values diversity, is able to show love openly through touch, and does not fear mistakes but learns from them. This is the description of a healthy community or family. By contrast, when the environment is characterized by twisted communication, inflexible rules, criticism for nonconformity, punishment for mistakes, no responsibility for promises made but not delivered, people feel worthless and are likely to develop self-destructive behavior. Therapists and spiritual directors tell us that it is possible, no matter how bad or how late, to raise one's self-esteem. In fact, they stake their living on it. Since feelings of low self-worth were learned, they can be unlearned. Something new takes the place of the old.

Some benefits from increasing a healthy sense of self include these:

1. A person who does not value herself expects someone else—husband, children, job—to bestow that value. When it is not forthcoming, she often turns to manipulation to get what she needs (including, incredibly, illness, perhaps to death).

2. Nothing is more sexually attractive than self-confidence.

3. One who is able to love himself is able to love others with a surer sense of what is appropriate.

4. One who has no firm center holds others responsible for his actions, becoming interchangeably subservient and tyrannical, while blaming others for his violence or ineffectiveness.

5. Those who do not love themselves give away their power and can be made to do anything by unscrupulous people.

6. The stronger one's self-worth, the easier it is to change and celebrate change in others.[3]

To sustain one's hard-won articulation of what is the truth about oneself, it would be beneficial to write and say frequently a "creed" of beliefs about one's individual worth. For any person serious about development in sexual-spiritual well-being, this would be a good beginning. Sarah Maney, a local poet, has expressed this truth lyrically, and as itself a prayer.

On the day I was born, God danced.
Did you really, God?
Was it a ritualistic, dignified,
bow-from-the-waist kind of dance?
Or was it just possibly a wild and crazy
arm-flinging kind of thing?
Did you pronounce somberly
that here was another "good girl"
that you have created?

Or did you yell and holler and
grab the guy on the corner
to let him know that this time
you had really done it!
This time you created a winner—
This one was going to go all the way!

I hope you did, God . . .
I really hope you did.

FRIENDSHIP

It may seem odd to put friendship in the context of strategies for spiritual growth and ministries for sexual integration. As that form of relationship, however, with which people have the most and longest familiarity, friendship is likely to have been the subject of more sustained reflection, prayer, and effort than sexual activity ever commanded. In Christian theology the notion of friendship, important to Greek thought as a component of self-understanding, seems to have been superceded by the concept of *agape*. The early Christians referred to each other not as friends but as brethren, which may have been thought more intimate and warm, as well as more appropriate by analogy to their relationship to the God of Jesus whose agapic love extended to all. Because friendship is selective and reciprocal, it lost out to *agape,* the requirement for more universal and unconditional love, in the development of early theological and liturgical language. But it may be time to rethink the issue and add friendship language more directly to the language of spirituality. I would like to propose that the primary vocation of the person is to friendship, and the many forms of ministry are ways to live out that mandate by service and action within a community of acquaintances, friends, and lovers. When relationships are the result of mutual will and desire, there is no victimization or fear of being taken over by the other. This would seem to be appropriate in our time as a mode of functioning for people who recognize their ultimate call as to friendship and know love to be an end in itself.

The dynamism of spirit is shown in the fact that friendships change with individuals' rhythmic needs for solitude and togetherness. They also are affected by the redefinition of boundaries which necessarily takes place as life goes on. An ability to express one's own needs for companionship corresponds with cycles of forgetting and rediscovering those needs. It is not surprising that the dynamic of our friendships—the reclaiming of the old ones and nurturing of the new—gives us a picture, perhaps better than our sexual histories, of our capacity both to give and to receive. The differences in our personalities are celebrated rather than muted in our friendships. Intimate conversation, even when not frequent, is both enjoyable and necessary; with a friend vulnerability can be expressed without putting us in the kind of danger of being hurt that sexual intimacy, even at its best, carries. It is an invitation to come to know, in a mirrorlike encounter, the inner self that does not easily reveal itself in more direct ways. If we listen with an inner ear to our conversations with our friends, we may learn not only something of our facility with the virtue of friendship but also something of our heart's desire with regard to the whole of life.

What are the functions of friendship? Are they capable of crossing gender lines? Do our capacities change as we go through different stages of life? The functions of friendship might be listed as follows:

1. To provide an atmosphere of trust as we experiment with self-revelation and intimacy. Friendship is important for self-knowledge. Through "another self" we gain a sense of our own significance.
2. To provide experience in the various depths and kinds of relationships. Friendship is important for self-fulfillment. Who we are is increased as we express ourselves in the variety of ways and roles evoked by specific friends.

3. To learn how to establish boundaries, allowing them to dissolve and appropriately reform. Friendship is important for self-transcendence. By taking us beyond the dependence of child-parent relationships as well as the unrelenting autonomy of adult-adult relationships in the world of work, we are prepared to accept the challenge of interdependence as central to a sense of who human beings are called to be.

4. To gain support and joy from those who have common interests and problems. Friendship is important to show us that service to others with an expectation of mutuality is healthy, and can give us an experiential reference from which to identify forms of the unhealthy emotional dependence that has come to be called "co-dependence."

These four functions suggest that the "school of friendship" can indeed be a school of personal and spiritual growth.

Some current research[4] has suggested that there is information about friendship, gathered from the studies of social scientists, that may help to clarify some aspects of the effects that our friendships have, not just on our spiritual growth but on our sexual lives as well. Significantly teenage girls tend to choose friends whose sexual attitudes and behavior are similar to their own. What has so often been deplored as peer pressure, may, when looked at from this point of view, be the tendency to join with those of common values and like-minded preferences. For teen boys, friendships with girls are used as a step toward dating. When the dating stage is entered, generally boys' commitment to friendships with other boys lessens. Girls, by contrast, maintain their same-sex friendships throughout dating relationship and often into adulthood. College women and men are similar to teens in friendship patterns, preferring a close friend to a group of casual acquaintances. Not surprisingly, friends are more important in the lives of young adults than for any other age group studied.

Research suggests that, in friendships with women, men tend to hide their weaknesses, while women hide their strengths. Women have been socialized to express more emotion than men. Early conclusions, that men do not disclose intimate knowledge about themselves to other men, appear to be challenged by later studies. Almost incredibly, 75 percent of married couples in a recent study said their spouse was their best friend. That may leave room for a more and a less sanguine interpretation. It could mean that in three out of four cases, lovers are in addition friends, thus experiencing at the same time with the same person some of the most transcendent experiences of intimacy available to human beings. On the other hand, it could mean that, in three out of four cases, the partners in marriage so take each other for granted that they seek no other companionship and expect the spouse to fill in for the lack of any other friendships. Marriage appears to increase the preference for same-sex friends, although that tendency is more pronounced among women than men.

How closely do friendship patterns adhere to the rules of conformity to gender role? During their mid-thirties, when most people are establishing their families, they are most likely to conform closely to culturally appropriate sex-role behavior. Men (about 50 percent) report that cross-sex friendships are often sexually motivated and some believe that sexual intimacy contributes to psychological closeness. By mid-life (thirties to age sixty) men again spend more time in groups than with individual friends. Their number of friends would have decreased as their emotional energy was directed to one person, usually a spouse. They seem to find making new friends increasingly difficult. Conversation appears to center in sports, work, and other external activities, not in personal themes or problems. Neither men nor women of middle age see sex and sexual concerns as topics of conversation, though women in mid-life spend more time with individual friends and talk about more personal topics. Friendships with the opposite sex for women shrink to about half the number of their earlier years; where relationships with men do continue, the women are generally employed, married to white-collar men, and belong to professional and recreational associations. Whether because of the cultural influence of the women's movement or for other more traditional reasons, middle-aged women have mostly same-sex friends.

As men and women move into older adulthood (their sixties and beyond), friendships become increasingly important, though, like teens, they face so much change that most find it hard to make new friends. Some patterns change at this stage of life. There is less confrontation in their relationships, and apparently less need for similarity of interests, personalities, and even values. This suggests that the elderly may enjoy the widest variety of interaction and intensity of any time of their lives. It may also underline the fact that wisdom and spiritual growth tend to show themselves in greater openness of the person, a wider horizon, and an increased tolerance for diversity. Women are more likely than men to replace a close friend who dies or is relocated. Such experience, as well as better communication skills and coping strategies, also appears to make adjustment to the loss of a spouse easier for women.

These selected items of information should not be read, however, to establish great differences in value or capacity for friendship between men and women. Actually more differences were found to be present between age groups than between the genders. Where friendships between women and men are inhibited, it is likely to be from close adherence to cultural expectations. Nonconventional men and women, defined as those more willing to take risks and seek greater pleasure or happiness, desiring to influence change and to exert more control over their lives, appear, according to researcher Robert Bell, to be more willing to reveal themselves in all their friendships, with members of the same and opposite sex. They see sexuality as less of a threat to male-female friendship than conventional persons do. They are less limited by cultural projections, including the fear of being labeled gay or lesbian. Flexibility and the willingness to shed gender roles can result in more satisfying relationships for both men and women. The refusal to seek pleasure is just as far from integration as the inability to choose anything but pleasure. A prior ordering that is neither rigid nor thoughtless belongs to the adult. Once the needs for food, clothing, and shelter have been met, the human striving for spiritual self-realization can expand through all the stages of life. What spiritually aware people need to do is to choose the particular areas of activity which can contribute both to their own development and, meaningfully, to society. The Christian call to mission is not just to work as service, but to membership in a community. Play, recovered in adult friendship, suggests the greater freedom of the spiritual person who can now act without utilitarian motive, rather, spontaneously from an inner response to the call for presence. In the words of Aelred of Rievaulx, a medieval bishop enjoying a revival precisely because of his writing on friendship, "In human affairs nothing more sacred is striven for, nothing more useful is sought after, nothing more difficult is discovered, nothing more sweet experienced, and nothing more profitable possessed. For friendship bears fruit in this life and in the next."

Ministry is not just *diaconia* (service); it is based primarily in *koinonia* (friendship).

MINISTRY OF AND TO PEOPLE WITH AIDS

In the form of what has been called the first "planetary"[5] illness, there is contained a challenge and an opportunity for every level of spiritual ministry: personal, communal, and professional. Among the many issues that could be discussed are four that will provide my focus for this reflection. (1) Because AIDS combines two of the most fearful realities, sex and death, it is doubly necessary and doubly difficult to deal with it as precisely an illness, rather than as a scourge of God to be magically forestalled by the ritual calling up of a scapegoat. (2) Because the population of gay men in the United States was the first to be massively affected by the HIV virus, it is important to separate the issues: compassion for those overtaken by illness and the tendency to reject them as symbols of our own vulnerability, fallibility, and mortality. (3) Because the American value for personal privacy and individual rights is so well developed, this challenge offers important and painful opportunities to conoider the correlative, but less-appreciated value for the common good. (4) Because professional health care workers and religious ministers to the sick and dying are, often for the first time in memory, facing choices that carry real though slim possibilities of infection, their practice of ministry calls them to rethink its transcendent meaning within the community.

The statistics about people with full-blown cases of AIDS, as well as projections about the numbers carrying the HIV virus and characterizations of high-risk behavior, are well known and readily available elsewhere. A recent survey of the teenage heterosexual population, generally regarded to be the subgroup at most risk as the trend toward heterosexual transmission increases, indicated that sexually active teenagers are aware of the major modes of HIV transmission, but they carry some misconceptions about transmission through casual contact. A large majority indicated fear of getting AIDS. They are, however, aware of the need for information and education and express interest in gaining a higher level of education. Where and how such education can be made available is a key question. Those who are aware of the real situation are challenged to address it. At present it is unlikely that religious education, in the form of confirmation preparation or Bible study or prayer and social action groups, is in the forefront of the effort to provide usable education to the population at large. Family-planning clinics have been found to be one of the few places that have regular opportunities to teach, discuss, and counsel adolescents on behavior changes necessary to prevent transmission of HIV. Most clinics have educational programs on conception control and sexually transmitted diseases, which have been or can be expanded to include content specific to AIDS. The role of IV drug use, the risks associated with having multiple partners, and methods available to reduce the risk of transmission, such as the use of condoms, are the most obvious of the lessons to be incorporated.

While it is efficient to use systems already in place for new learning, it seems to me that to eschew an active role in AIDS education is to neglect a moment that could be of great significance to the integration of sexuality and spirituality in our religious lives and institutions.

The challenge of doubled fear

AIDS has been described as "diabolical," "malignant," "more subtle and more insidious than medieval leprosy, Renaissance syphilis, or machine-age tuberculosis."[6] It has become, following the disclosure that this disease is linked to sex, blood, and drugs, a metaphor for our time. Some of the more hysterical responses have pictured it as having come into our orderly world from another one entirely, a less moral world, a world in which illness should not be viewed as the inevitable lot of finite being co-existing in finite space, but as the direct result of sin. The successful avoidance of the disease, following the same presuppositions, stands as direct testimony of virtue. It is of course not new to human beings to equate sickness with evil and to labor to produce theoretical models of the relationship between the two. What is different here, and calls for refutation, is the tendency to smear all of sexual interaction with the fear of death and contagion. What the metaphors of violence surrounding sex have not been able to do to profane sex by abuse, the metaphor of disease is likely to do. It sometimes appears that people think if they do not contract AIDS (or perhaps cancer), they will never die. The profound levels of truth in the connection between sex and death are betrayed and falsified by this literal and reductionist level of allegation. "I'm glad I don't have teenagers to raise now" . . . "I'm glad I'm no longer on the dating scene" are comments that are not only isolationist, but forgetful. The deepest truth about sexuality is that it is always dangerous. The common sense about sexuality is that it is not more dangerous now, to the responsible human person, than it has ever been. The routes of transmission of HIV are controllable. Ever so, the lesson is much larger: heavy burdens await us whenever our actions disturb the "dynamic equilibria between humans, their physical surroundings, and the totality of living beings."[7]

To confront and challenge the process by which a sexually transmitted disease becomes a symbol of evil and its overcoming produces scapegoating of classes of people considered marginal and "foreign" requires education that is more of the imagination than of reason. This is precisely the form of education for which religious and spiritual traditions have great expertise and credibility. This crisis can be a challenge to do once more what only religion is able to do: to help people love more perfectly. But more than that: to love in the face of the realization that death is inevitable.

Compassion

As one becomes aware of the size and seriousness of the disease of AIDS, there must be more to concern oneself with than the avoidance of contagion. This is an issue for us all because precautions must be learned and taken so that the person survives. But it is not the only issue. To avoid contact with those who are ill, beyond the requirement of reasonable care for life and health, is a temptation. It is to say: *I am not one of them.* It polarizes and alienates some from the others. We project our deepest fears of vulnerability onto those who are suffering the most and who least deserve to be abandoned. Of the many meanings that have been attached to the ancient rites of anointing the sick, at least one of them is to mark and maintain the centrality of the person who is ill, even ill unto death, as a place of sacramental proclamation and grace for the community. The person who is confronting his own mortality, not now symbolically through religious rites of initiation, but literally in the grip of death, is identified more, not less closely, with the archetypal figure of Christ. When that person is able to embody such a powerful symbolic meaning, not only is the suffering more bearable, but he becomes a locus for the whole community to celebrate the deepest mystery it knows: that ineffably, through death comes life, and through (not from) suffering comes transformation.

Compassion, therefore, has a long and rich spiritual history. It has little to do with pity and much to do with reverence and fellow feeling. Compassion empowers the onlooker as much as it empowers the subject undergoing the particular suffering that engulfs her. There is healing going on here: healing that may or may not be related to a cure of the disease. The healing of self and healing of society is the work of compassion.

But some, very tender-hearted and caring people, have said: How can I feel compassion for those who succumb to AIDS? It's different. They asked for it. By their actions, they have broken rules. If I care for them, am I not condoning what they have done? This sort of question comes out of an extraordinary contempt for vulnerability, it seems to me. No one has, will, or should ask another human being to correspond perfectly to their sense of righteousness as the price of compassion. Reverence for the dignity of the person is prior to anything the person does or deserves. Moreover, the compassion urged upon his followers by Jesus was not based upon deserving but upon the divine model of unconditional forgiveness and care. Not because the lepers or Samaritans or prostitutes or tax collectors had acted in such a way to gain his contingent approval but because his Father allowed the rain to fall upon the just and the unjust: this was Jesus' motivation for responding out of his gift and opportunity to their need. His model of compassion is particularly eloquent in that he also expressed his need to them and was served in turn. A shared meal, a tearful sign of affection and sorrow, the respect of a straight answer: these were things he asked and accepted as proportionate to the forgiveness of sins, return of sight to the blind, and restoration of health. The person who fears that a response of affection to someone who has not kept all the rules will shatter her own fragile resolve has more need than the patient for the opportunity to imitate the unconditioned love of the Holy One. Love means, in effect, I want you *to be*. In this, divine and human compassion coincide.

Balancing individual rights with the common good

While a multitude of ethical issues can be defined in the debates about the social ramifications of the AIDS pandemic, one that is particularly significant for personal and communal spirituality is that of the individual's privacy versus the right of others to know. The basic connectedness, that is, the spiritual truth of the human race, is performed most dramatically in our sexual interactions.

The case of the so-called Patient Zero of the Soviet Union, the first man through whom the AIDS virus infiltrated that country, is instructive.

> The first known patient, citizen K., aged thirty-five, lived in an east African country in 1981 and over a period of several months had homosexual contacts with a native. Vacationing in his own country and enjoying a brief liaison with a Russian in November 1981, K had passive anal sex with a bisexual African in March 1982. That summer he began to experience mild fevers accompanied with headache, insomnia, and respiratory distress, followed by blood-tinged diarrhea. When routine examinations failed to explain his clinical picture, K was repatriated and spent five months in a Moscow hospital. The physicians there noticed his generalized lymphadenopathy and proposed a diagnosis of Crohn's disease, a form of chronic inflammatory bowel disorder. No one thought of AIDS. The patient returned to his hometown and, between summer 1983 and 1986, indulged in homosexual relationships with twenty-two partners. In 1984 he had a bout of chronic pneumonia and two crops of shingles; toward the end of 1985 he manifested Kaposi's sarcoma. The diagnosis of AIDS was not made until toward the end of 1986, whereupon the public health authorities undertook, in January 1987, a rigorous epidemiologic inquiry.
>
> K's twenty-two partners were tracked down. They all denied having had homosexual relationships outside of those with "Patient Zero," but admitted heterosexual contacts. They were young men eighteen to twenty years old. None considered himself homosexual and, until January 1987, none had ever heard of AIDS. Tests showed that five of these twenty-two partners were seropositive. Each of them had had heterosexual contacts with several women, on the average five. Only two had transmitted the infection to their partners, the first to a single woman, the second to two. The latter, though only weakly seropositive, sparked a tragic chain reaction: on the one hand, his blood was used to transfuse six recipients, of whom five became seropositive; on the other hand, one of the women he infected gave birth to a sick infant while the other gave blood for the treatment of a hemophiliac (who remained negative eleven months after the transfusion). From an epidemiologic as well as a sociocultural point of view, it is interesting to note that one of the seropositive had anal sex with two women who desired thereby to retain their virginity; neither of these women was infected.[8]

This description, precisely because of the graphic detail and objective language with which it is drawn, is somewhat shocking. It describes a web of involvement and damage that continues to expand. While this case is taken from records regarding the Soviet Union, the United States has still the most heavily infected population in the world. When the actions of one person affect the life and vitality of another person, as sexual actions always do, it is clear that here is a matter of social justice and personal responsibility, not only or perhaps even primarily an issue of individual rights.

Qualities of effective ministry

Not every priest, chaplain, or commissioned minister probably can or should deal with people with AIDS. Even as professionals, ministers have different levels of being able to cope with things like the fear of the unknown and fear of contagion. People are at different points in their moral development, which enables them to acknowledge the possibility of goodness coinciding with actions they consider wrong, or badness with appearances they consider good. People have had different experiences of death, so that they may not yet in their relational and spiritual lives, have had occasion to overcome the denial of death and powerlessness that is buried so deep under the surface in many young adults. Levels of homophobia may have been acquired through cultural or family systems and may not have been exorcized by their understanding of Christian love; homophobia may even be exacerbated by the minister's accession to a role that carries prestige and authority in the community. There are some who should probably not attempt personal ministry to people with AIDS because they are inclined to identify excessively with those who suffer. Their anger at the injustice of it, their frustration at the impossibility of alleviating such pain could make them useless or even harmful to those they wish to help. Those who have a great need for "omnipotence" in their chosen profession, whether medical or religious, are not likely to be catalysts of the healing and spiritual growth that are possible. "What we're finding," wrote a founder and director of a program to help persons with AIDS, "is that if the doctor, nurse—whoever—are really there to take care of the patient, when the patient is healed, they're thrilled. If they're really there to take care of their own needs, when the patient becomes responsible, stops acting like a victim, they're devastated. It's like you took their job away."[9]

But it should not be inferred that only those with very special gifts and callings ought to aspire to ministry to people with AIDS. Anyone who understands and anticipates these issues should be able to serve effectively without harming others or themselves. By identifying one's own particular vulnerabilities, one is already in a process of discernment that will be essential to the ongoing process of reading the needs and opportunities within a situation in relation to one's own gifts and skills. Such ministers will then be able to seek proper information and, with sensitivity and self-control, apply it.

The fruits of grace experienced in such a ministry can be far in excess of the particular time, energy, or skill of a single person, when a peer or volunteer support system is set up with the appropriate supervision and motivation.

Among the many means reported as effective by those who have been catalysts for personal and spiritual healing is the creation and reinforcement of a positive self-image. Illness of any kind is threatening to body image and self-esteem. Whatever builds the sense of being an active center of worth strengthens the immune system and the spirit. Some have found that the commitment to community, sometimes for the first time in a person's life, makes a significant difference to the way they are able to live while undergoing the unpredictable course of such disease. Among the many meanings of the ancient Christian ritual of the anointing of the sick is the acknowledgement that the person among us who is overtaken by illness, perhaps in the very grip of death, is the one whose being most closely manifests to all the paradigmatic value of the Christ-figure. This communal perception transfers to the individual who can then identify herself, now not only symbolically with the journey from death to transformed life of Christ, but also literally, in time and space, experiencing the centrality of that mystery. The one who suffers becomes the locus for the community to proclaim, in fact to celebrate, the ultimacy of its commitment to life. It can become an occasion to recognize the face of the Holy One in what would otherwise be ineffable and terrifying. This discovery has on occasion led to a process through which communities have been able to celebrate previously neglected or misunderstood steps in their spiritual journeys. A renaming can produce a new grasp of the spiritual significance of sexual identity, a new peace with real spiritual experiences. In some quite unexpected ways the experience with AIDS and people who have AIDS has fostered new spiritual maturity among ministers and their clients. Some have reported that a growing sense of a shared history has come out of the prayer, dialog, and liturgy of those who are meeting this challenge. They are laying claim to their own symbols and rituals, and in the words of one, have "reclaimed God from being the property of moral insiders."

Whether the ministry is carried on by insiders or outsiders, there are specific things that persons with AIDS need from those who would minister to them:

1. An understanding of the prejudices, social barriers, and stresses they will invariably encounter. This is of importance not only for those with actual diagnosis of the disease but also for those who are still well but worried about their chances.

2. Information and encouragement toward abstinence in new sexual relationships and responsibility with regard to partners. This is problematic for

anyone who has internalized the taboo about discussing explicit or nonconventional sexual matters.

3. Information on government and privately sponsored programs for financial aid or assistance. Homelessness and unemployment are sometimes more distressing day-by-day problems than the physical symptoms of the illnesses.

4. Availability for counseling at the time of diagnosis and at other times of depression when suicide may appear to be the best way to deal with a desperate situation. Especially when families are no longer available to patients or when social stigma has cut them off from normal support groups, it is practically a necessity of life that there be someone for them to turn to immediately, at any time of day.

5. Nonjudgmental support. The more isolated and marginalized a group becomes, the more important that they feel a sense of belonging.

6. Support for friends and family, especially intimate partners of those with AIDS. Doctors have noted that the patients who survive the longest generally have families with a strong commitment to their care and nutrition and the will to participate no matter what it takes. What it takes may be easier with the support of the minister. For partners, the grieving process is made easier when it can be done not in isolation but in a way that has some reference to the ongoing community of the living.

7. Self-care. The ministers themselves face feelings of frustration and failure. Some begin to distance themselves not from fear of contagion but from emotional weariness. Those who have been effective say that it is important to see oneself not as one who heals or resolves the problems, but as one who helps to make the patient's life more full and significant. The most ancient secret for dealing with stress is contained in the concept of the sabbath: rest, relaxation, good food, intimate relationships, laughter.

It is without doubt that our social and cultural response to this disease and the persons who contract it will be deeply influenced by our ability or inability to deal with sexuality as body and spirit and it will test our capacity for justice and compassion.

Conclusion

I have tried to argue that there is a connection between sexuality and spirituality. It cannot be one of identity (sexuality is spirituality) for that is to say more than the truth and it does not hold up through long analysis. Such an overstatement is not without value, however, for it jolts people out of the equally fallacious assumption that sexuality and spirituality are mutually exclusive. The relation between them can be conceptualized as that of sacrament, in which the sensual action, intelligibly though not visibly, produces effects in the spiritual order. The real connection takes place, of course, not in abstract concepts, but in individual lives. Therefore I have tried to illustrate moments in sexual and spiritual growth through the stories of individuals making sense of their own experiences.

The attempt of this book has been to affirm a process and an attitude toward the sexual life. It is simultaneously the expression of human being in its relationship to the absolute and the expression of that place in our depths where bonds between persons are formed. Interpersonal love has been found to have a mystical and unifying dimension. The new sexuality is not divine (encouraging a cult of sex), nor demonic (a fear of sex), but human.

Sexuality, it has been shown, is a new source of religious experience. Just how rich that source will be remains to be seen in the lives of people who live out their sexual potential as a spiritual journey. In addition, sexuality can be, by reason of its power to center and liberate more persons in more and more ways, a contributing factor to the renewal of social and cultural life. The revolutionary potential here depends not so much on the living but on the telling. Renaming is contagious. It can bring sexuality and spirituality into sacramental relation for increasing numbers of people, which is, in fact, a new cultural reality. It will not be without problems, but the human spirit has never preferred to live with its old problems rather than to attempt to solve them, appropriately calculating risk and benefit. The new awareness can become a new connectedness through one's own sexual potential to a humankind aware of its power, no longer in dualistic conflict, but in wholeness (purity) of heart, and committed to the fullest development of all. Then it might become capable of accepting its responsibility for the new creation: a seamless robe of love, woven in the Spirit.

Notes

For each chapter I have cited some general works which have been important in the development of my thought, followed by specific citations in the order that they appear in my text.

INTRODUCTION

Foucault, Michel. *Technologies of the Self.* Amherst: University of Massachusetts Press, 1988.

Lensing, George S. *Wallace Stevens: A Poet's Growth.* Baton Rouge: Louisiana State University Press, 1986.

Levine, Donald N. *The Flight from Ambiguity: Essays in Social and Cultural Theory.* Chicago: University of Chicago Press, 1985.

Ricoeur, Paul. "The Model of the Text: Meaningful Action Considered as a Text." Chap. 8 in his *Hermeneutics and the Human Sciences,* edited, translated, and introduced by John B. Thompson. Cambridge: Cambridge University Press, 1981.

Stevens, Wallace. *The Collected Poems.* New York: Vintage Books, 1990.

1. Stevens, *The Collected Poems,* p. 520.

2. *Anamnesis* is a term from eucharistic theology. From the Greek, literally "not forgetting," it has come to mean the dynamic and participatory "remembering" of Jesus' words "Do this in memory of me." Some scholars insist that in the Psalms and other Hebrew Scripture usage the one who is called upon to remember is God, who never forgets the divine mercy and his faithfulness. Moreover, God remembers the mighty works of deliverance by doing them again in each generation. Who and what is remembered, that is, made present again, in the eucharistic liturgy is still a disputed question, worthy of renewed discussion. As used in this context, *anamnesis* calls for a remembering of a sacred dimension of sexuality that is also dynamic and participatory. The difference would be that in thinking about sex as *anamnesis,* one would be thinking about calling upon God to remember the self-gift given in creation.

3. Foucault, *Technologies of the Self,* p. 10.

CHAPTER 1: REAL SEXUALITY AND OTHER CONCEPTS

Brown, Peter. *The Body and Society: Men, Women and Renunciation in Early Christianity.* New York: Columbia University Press, 1988.

————. *Religion and Society in the Age of Augustine.* New York: Harper and Row, 1972.

Brownmiller, Susan. *Femininity.* New York: Fawcett Columbine, 1984.

Bullough, Vern, and Bonnie Bullough. *Sin, Sickness, and Sanity: A History of Sexual Attitudes.* New American Library, 1977.

Connell, R. W. *Gender and Power: Society, the Person, and Sexual Politics.* Stanford University Press, 1987.

Francoeur, Robert T. *Becoming a Sexual Person.* New York: John Wiley and Sons, 1984.

Foucault, Michel. *The History of Sexuality. Vol. 1, An Introduction.* New York: Random House, 1978.

Pagels, Elaine. *Adam, Eve, and the Serpent.* New York: Vintage Books, 1988.

Ricoeur, Paul. "The Model of the Text: Meaningful Action Considered As a Text." Chap. 8 in his *Hermeneutics and the Human Sciences,* edited, translated, and introduced by John B. Thompson. Cambridge: Cambridge University Press, 1981.

Rilke, Rainer Maria. *Duino Elegies.* Translated by J. B. Leishman and Stephen Spender. New York: W. W. Norton, 1967.

Spohn, William C., S.J. "The Reasoning Heart: An American Approach to Christian Discernment," *Theological Studies* 30–52.

Scheler, Max. "Ordo Amoris." In *Collected Writings.* Evanston: Northwestern University Press, 1978.

Wainwright, Geoffrey. "Types of Spirituality." In *The Study of Spirituality,* edited by Cheslyn Jones, Geoffrey Wainwright, and Edward Yarnold, S.J. New York: Oxford University Press, 1986, 592–605.

1. On body as subject and object: Maurice Merleau-Ponty, *The Primacy of Perception,* ed. with introduction by James M. Edie (Evanston: Northwestern University Press, 1964), pp. 162–64.

2. Paul Ricoeur develops the dialectic of understanding and explanation in *Hermeneutics and the Human Sciences,* pp. 210–21.

3. Even Foucault's *History of Sexuality* is not an example of this. I refer to narratives of events or actions that give insight into the meanings and interelationships of those events. Foucault is tracking the "deployment" of an ideology. To some extent the history of heterosexual male sexuality has been written, in which female sexuality is included as unchanging object upon which, as upon nature, male agency is exercised. The inclusion of women's subjective naming of their own experience has required that assumptions about the "nature of" human sexuality be revised. This premise is in direct contradiction to that expressed by Camille Paglia: "Sexuality is a murky realm of contradiction and ambivalence. . . . It cannot be 'fixed' by codes of social or moral convenience, whether from the political left or right. For nature's fascism is greater than that of any society. There is a daemonic instability in sexual relations that we may have to accept" (Paglia, *Sexual Personae* [New Haven: Yale University Press, 1990], p. 13). Those who see sexuality as nothing but incorrigible instinct, which locks us inescapably in chthonian nature, would consider such "history-telling" to be ridiculous, if not impossible.

4. All Scripture quotes are from *The New Oxford Annotated Bible,* Revised Standard Version (New York: Oxford University Press, 1977).

5. On the use of the feminine pronoun for Holy Spirit: Farrelly, *God's Work in the World*, p. 71 concludes that there is every biblical and theological reason that the feminine images of the Holy Spirit should be acknowledged by the immediate and universal use of the feminine form of in references to the Third Person of the Trinity.

6. On spirituality in the women's movement: *The Politics of Women's Spirituality: Essays on the Rise of Spiritual Power Within the Feminist Movement*, ed. Charlene Spretnak (New York: Doubleday, 1982), especially pp. 370–85.

7. Solovyov, *Sexual Love and Western Morality*, ed. D. P. Verene (New York: Harper and Row, 1972), p. 252.

8. On "mystical" in the Eastern Church: Thomas Hopko, *The Spirit of God* (Wilton, Ct: Morehouse-Barlow, 1976), p. 33.

9. Rilke, *Duino Elegies*, p. 107.

10. Ibid., p. 123.

CHAPTER 2: THE SEXUALITY OF JESUS AND THE HUMAN VOCATION

Brownmiller, Susan. *Femininity.* New York: Fawcett Columbine, 1984.

Connell, R. W. *Gender and Power: Society, The Person and Sexual Politics.* Palo Alto: Stanford University Press, 1987.

Fuchs, Josef, S.J. *Christian Morality: The Word Becomes Flesh.* Translated by Brian McNeil. Washington, D.C.: Georgetown University Press, 1987.

James, William. *The Varieties of Religious Experience.* Edited with Introduction by Martin E. Marty. New York: Penguin Books, 1982.

Lerner, Gerda. *The Creation of Patriarchy.* New York: Oxford University Press, 1986.

Mackin, Theodore, S.J. *The Marital Sacrament: Marriage in the Catholic Church.* New York: Paulist, 1989.

Nelson, James. *The Intimate Connection: Male Sexuality, Masculine Spirituality.* Philadelphia, Westminster Press, 1988.

Schillebeeckx, Edward. *Jesus: An Experiment in Christology.* New York: Crossroad, 1981.

Steinberg, Leo. *The Sexuality of Christ in Renaissance Art and in Modern Oblivion.* New York: Pantheon, 1983.

Tyrrell, Thomas. *Urgent Longing: Reflections on the Experience of Infatuation, Human Intimacy, and Contemplative Love.* Whitinsville, MA: Affirmation Books, 1980.

1. On the ways in which different generations and cultures have appropriated Jesus for their own times: Jaroslav Pelikan, *Jesus Through the Centuries: His Place in the History of Culture* (New Haven: Yale University Press, 1985).

2. On 1 Corinthians 7 as interpretation of what matters above all: See Josef Fuchs, *Christian Morality*, pp. 84–101. Fuchs shows Paul as answering those in Corinth who believed the Christians should change their normal lifestyle: ". . . each should live the life which the Lord has assigned to him, and in which God has called him. This is my rule in all the churches" (v. 17), and Fuchs comments: "One who believes that, as a Christian, he must alter his lifestyle, has not yet grasped that it is belonging to Christ that matters, and that in comparison to this any particular lifestyle is simply not important" (p. 84). Verse 7, especially the phrase *per indulgentiam* or *per veniam*, was interpreted by St. Augustine not as concession, but as forgiveness, and implied for him that where forgiveness is required sin must exist. It follows that

when married people come together in order to escape the danger of fornication, rather than because of procreation—which was for Augustine the only aim of marital union—there necessarily exists (at least venial) sin. This understanding of St. Augustine, based on questionable exegesis, determined the Christian teaching on marriage for many centuries. It gave relatively few married people the chance to belong wholly to the Lord (p. 87).

3. For Clement's discussion: *Stromata 3*, 49, in *Alexandrian Christianity*, vol. 2, pp. 40–92, in The Library of Christian Classics, trans. J. Oulton and H. Chadwick (Philadelphia, 1954).

4. Augustine, *The City of God Against the Pagans*, Book XIV, XXIII in Loeb Classical Library, IV, trans. Philip Levine (Cambridge, MA: Harvard University Press, 1966), pp. 379–85.

Thomas Aquinas, *Summa Theologica* 3, q. 14, a. 4; q. 15, a. 2, in *Summa Theologica*, vol. 2 (New York: Benziger, 1947), pp. 2104, 2106.

5. Symeon the New Theologian: *Ethical Treatises* 1, 6; in Wainwright, *The Study of Spirituality*, p. 241.

6. I am aware that this assertion contradicts the position elaborated by Michel Foucault, who wrote: "We are often reminded of the countless procedures which Christianity once employed to make us detest the body; but let us ponder all the ruses that were employed for centuries to make us love sex, to make the knowledge of it desirable and everything said about it precious. . . . These devices are what ought to make us wonder today. Moreover, we need to consider the possibility that one day, perhaps, in a different economy of bodies and pleasures, people will no longer quite understand how the ruses of sexuality . . . were able to subject us to that austere monarchy of sex" (*History of Sexuality*, vol. 1, p. 159). He finds not "liberation" but enslavement in the explicitation of sexual symbols. Perhaps in another situation I would agree. For the present, the absence of sexual referents in religious symbols is indeed one of the factors that account for women undervaluing their own being.

7. Once-born and twice-born personality types are described in *The Varieties of Religious Experience*, pp. 80, 139–44, 239 n. 2. People of the former personality type are those for whom adjustments to life have been straightforward and whose lives have been more or less a peaceful flow from the moment of their births. The twice-borns, on the other hand, have not had an easy time of it. Their lives are marked by a continual struggle to attain some sense of order. Unlike the once-borns, they cannot take things for granted. According to James, these personalities have different world views. For a once-born personality, the sense of self, as a guide to conduct and attitude, derives from a feeling of being at home and in harmony with one's environment. For a twice-born, the sense of self derives from a feeling of profound separateness. A sense of belonging becomes practically significant when individuals see themselves as perpetuating and strengthening existing institutions. They are in harmony with ideals of duty and responsibility. The sense of self flows easily to and from the outer world. Those who seek out or initiate change tend to be twice-born personalities, people who feel separate from their environment, including other people. They may work in organizations, but never belong to them. Their sense of who they are does not depend upon memberships, work roles, or other social indicators of identity. They search out ways to profoundly alter human relationships.

8. Tyrell, *Urgent Longing*, p. 52.

9. On the biochemistry of pleasure: Ron Rosenbaum, "The Chemistry of Love," *Esquire* 101/6 (June 1984) 100–111.

10. James Nelson attempts to offer a balanced approach to men's spirituality without homophobia, false guilt, or evasion of responsibility for structures. See *The Intimate Connection*.

11. On femininity and size: Susan Brownmiller, *Femininity*, p. 30; on diet, p. 50. An October 1991 newspaper report commented on the visit of Princess Diana to Pakistan. As Pakistan News columnist Asir Ajmal wrote: "Our otherwise tall and handsome Premier Nawa Sharif looked like a midget next to the royal guest. . . . If Britain is interested in maintaining ties it should choose its future princesses with care, especially when it comes to height."

12. The study on what women want in future gender relations is reported in Connell, *Gender and Power*, pp. 250–53.

CHAPTER 3: STAGES IN SEXUAL-SPIRITUAL GROWTH

Francoeur, Robert T. *Becoming a Sexual Person*. New York: John Wiley, 1984.

Hillesum, Etty. *An Interrupted Life: The Diaries of Etty Hillesum, 1941–1943*. New York: Pantheon Books, 1983.

Keen, Sam. *The Passionate Life: Stages of Loving*. New York: Harper and Row, 1983.

Sarrel, Lorna J., and Philip M. Sarrel. *Sexual Turning Points: The Seven Stages of Adult Sexuality*. New York: Macmillan, 1984.

Satir, Virginia. *The New Peoplemaking*. Mountain View, CA: Science and Behavior Books, 1988.

Sullivan, Susan, and Matthew Kawiak. *Parents Talk Love: A Catholic Family Handbook about Sex*. New York: Paulist, 1985.

Underhill, Evelyn. *The Life of the Spirit and the Life of Today*. New York: Harper and Row, 1986.

Washbourn, Penelope. "Body/World: The Religious Dimensions of Sexuality." *Christianity and Crisis* 34/21 (December 9, 1974) 279–84.

1. For a detailed illustration of the Kinsey scale (0 = entirely heterosexual to 6 = entirely homosexual), see Gary Kelly, *Sexuality Today*, pp. 280–82.

2. William Stayton, "A Theory of Sexual Orientation: The Universe As a Turn-On," *Topics in Clinical Nursing* 1/4 (1980) 1–7, used with author's permission.

3. Patrick Carnes, who coined the phrase "sexual addiction," reports finding that the personality profile of the one who is compulsive in sexual acting out is more inhibited and shame-based than sensually indulgent. It is different in kind, not degree, from "normal" sexual self-expression (*Out of the Shadows: Understanding Sexual Addiction* [Minneapolis: Comp Care Publishers, 1983]). See also the extensive writing of John Money, whose research into paraphilias of all sorts suggests that better early education, rather than a less permissive environment, is the answer to better sexual socialization.

4. Nelson, *The Intimate Connection*, p. 95.

5. On marriage as a sacrament, see Kasper, 126, 111–128 and Karl Rahner, "Considerations on the Active Role of the Person in the Sacramental Event," *Theological Investigations XIV*, trans. David Bourke (London: Darton, Longman & Todd; New York: Seabury 1976), p. 177.

6. As quoted in Underhill, *The Life of the Spirit and the Life of Today*, p. 42.

7. Both quotes on childbirth and liberation are from Penelope Washbourn, "Body/World," p. 282.

8. The practical problems of parenting today are illustrated by the following financial information. Costs for the first year of a baby's life have been tallied (Health Insurance Association of America) at $10,783: medical (parental and birth) $4,334; diapers (2,340 used)

$435; day care (fifty percent of all new mothers work) $4,000; feeding (bottles and solid food) $208; apparel $875; furniture (bed and bath) $606; accessories (for car, kitchen, and play) $325. On participation by men in childbirth: The latest rage among childbirth educators is the "empathy belly," a "35 pound, sweat-inducing, rib-crushing, back-swaying pregnancy simulator" that is used to educate men to the physical ramifications of pregnancy" (*Contemporary Sexuality Newsletter* 22/6 [June, 1990] 11).

9. It is impossible for people in our time to appreciate the submersion in reproductive role of past ages. Peter Brown describes the kind of society shown in a mid-fifth century text on the legend of St. Thecla, reflecting life in Seleucia, on the southern coast of Turkey. It was a "society more helplessly exposed to death than is even the most afflicted underdeveloped country in the modern world. Citizens of the Roman Empire at its height, in the second century A.D. were born into the world with an average life expectancy of less than twenty-five years. Death fell savagely on the young. Those who survived childhood remained at risk. Only four out of every one hundred men, and fewer women, lived beyond the age of fifty. In such a situation, only the privileged or the eccentric few could enjoy the freedom to do what they pleased with their sexual drives" (*Body and Society* [New York: Oxford, 1988], p. 6).

10. Kundera, *The Unbearable Lightness of Being*, p. 313.

11. On leadership and mentoring: Abraham Zaleznik, "Managers and Leaders: Are they different?" in *Contemporary Issues in Leadership*, ed. Rosenbach (New York: Mentor, 1958), pp. 99–100.

12. Hillesum, *An Interrupted Life*, p. 166.

13. John Dunne, *The Way of All the Earth* (Notre Dame, IN: University of Notre Dame Press, 1978), pp. 232, 233.

CHAPTER 4: CYCLES OF CHANGE

Douglas, Mary. *Purity and Danger: An Analysis of the Concepts of Pollution and Taboo.* London: Routledge and Kegan Paul, 1966.

Levine, Donald N. *The Flight from Ambiguity: Essays in Social and Cultural Theory.* Chicago: University of Chicago Press, 1985.

Sister Clare. *Journey out of Chaos.* Whitinsville, MA: Affirmation Books, 1981.

Turner, Brian S. *The Body and Society: Explorations in Social Theory.* New York: Basil Blackwell, 1984.

Underhill, Evelyn. *The Life of the Spirit and the Life of Today.* New York: Harper and Row, 1986.

1. On ritual forms of primitive peoples: Douglas, *Purity and Danger*, pp. 27–35.

2. On filtering mechanism: Douglas, *Purity and Danger*, p. 37; functions of threat of pollution: p. 133.

3. On anger and taboos: Sister Clare, *Journey out of Chaos*, p. 109.

4. Gordon, *Final Payments*, p. 163.

5. Douglas, *Purity and Danger*, p. 158.

6. Gordon, *Final Payments*, pp. 21, 22, 23, 256.

7. Douglas, *Purity and Danger*, p. 163.

8. Gordon, *Final Payments*, pp. 294–95.

9. Ibid., p. 289.

10. On defining anomaly: An anomaly is an element which does not fit a given set or series; ambiguity is a character of statements capable of two interpretations. Douglas, p. 37.

11. Gennep, *The Rites of Passage,* p. 26. Arnold van Gennep introduced the terminology of the three stages of ceremonies accompanying an individual's life crises: separation, transition, incorporation.

12. Rilke, *Duino Elegies,* p. 99 (dates as 1903).

13. On anorexia as a liminal state: Turner, *The Body and Society,* p. 113; quotes pp. 195, 197.

14. Food disorders as political problems: Thomas Szasz, *Law, Liberty, and Psychiatry* (New York: Macmillan, 1963), pp. 14–17, situates mental disorders as deviations from a defined norm and suggests the remedies are social, ethical, and political rather than medical.

15. Levine, *The Flight from Ambiguity,* p. 30.

16. Ibid., p. 31.

17. Hillesum, *An Interrupted Life,* p. 166.

18. Washbourn, "Body/World: The Religious Dimensions of Sexuality," p. 282.

CHAPTER 5: THEOLOGY OF SPIRIT

Bynum, Caroline Walker. *Jesus as Mother: Studies in the Spirituality of the High Middle Ages.* Berkeley: University of California Press, 1987.

Cahill, Lisa Sowle. "Catholic Sexual Ethics and the Dignity of the Person: A Double Message." *Theological Studies* 50 (1989) 120–50.

Coffey, David. "The 'Incarnation' of the Holy Spirit in Christ." *Theological Studies* 45 (1984) 466–81.

Congar, Yves. *The Word and the Spirit.* Translated by David Smith. San Francisco: Harper and Row, 1984.

Dunne, John S. *The Homing Spirit: A Pilgrimage of the Mind, of the Heart, of the Soul.* New York: Crossroad, 1987.

Fuchs, Josef, S.J.: *Christian Morality: The Word Becomes Flesh.* Translated by Brian McNeil. Washington, DC: Georgetown University Press, 1987.

Haight, Roger. "The Point of Trinitarian Theology." *Toronto Journal of Theology* 4/2 (1988) 191–204.

Hopko, Thomas. *The Spirit of God.* Wilton, CT: Morehouse-Barlow, 1976.

L'Engle, Madeleine. *The Irrational Season.* New York: Crossroad, 1977.

Mackin, Theodore, S.J. *The Marital Sacrament: Marriage in the Catholic Church.* New York: Paulist, 1989.

Mahoney, John, S.J. *The Making of Moral Theology.* Oxford: Clarendon Press, 1987.

McCormick, Richard A., S.J. "Moral Theology 1940–1989: An Overview." *Theological Studies* 50 (1989) 3–24.

McFague, Sallie. *Models of God: Theology for an Ecological, Nuclear Age.* Philadelphia: Fortress, 1987.

Quelquejeu, Bernard. "Diversity in Historical Moral Systems and a Criterion for Universality in Moral Judgment." In *Concilium 150, Christian Ethics: Uniformity, Universality,*

Pluralism, edited by Jacques Pohier and Dietmar Mieth (Edinburgh: T & T Clark, 1981), 47–53.

Rahner, Karl. *The Spirit in the Church.* New York: Seabury, 1979.

1. Dunne, *The Homing Spirit,* p. 22.
2. L'Engle, *The Irrational Season,* p. 171.
3. Dunne, *The Homing Spirit,* p. 41.
4. Hopko, *The Spirit of God,* p. 80.
5. L'Engle, *The Irrational Season,* p. 171.
6. Mackin, *The Marital Sacrament,* pp. 633–42.
7. Dunne, *The Homing Spirit,* p. 32.
8. Quoted in Congar, *The Word and the Spirit,* p. 86.
9. John Cassian is quoted in Hopko, *The Spirit of God,* p. 106, as is Isaac of Syria. The kind of sinful passion or "self-love" that is evil is that "which considers the body, the flesh, and the world as ends in themselves. . . . Christ came 'not to condemn the world but that the world through him might be saved' (John 3:17), . . . Salvation simply means genuine life. It is the knowledge of the truth in the proper vision *(theoria)* and action *(praxis)* of life. It does not happen or begin 'after we die' [but is] begun already now within the conditions of life in this world." Nor does it come "to human persons 'from outside' " as the arbitrary act of God alone. "[Salvation] requires the living action of human *persons,* by grace, in union with the action of God, so that God's action and human action become one theandric action, one co-action of the divine and the human. . . . Wherever and however a person does good, knows the truth, creates beauty, edifies creation, he or she does so by God's Spirit, and to this extent he or she is 'saved.' . . . Although such a person may not consciously be aware of it, he or she is in communion with God, through the Word and the Spirit, to the extent that he or she lives in goodness, in truth, and in love" (ibid., 108, 109, 110).
10. Hillesum, *An Interrupted Life,* pp. 172, 173.
11. Rahner, *The Spirit in the Church,* p. 6.
12. Kundera, *Unbearable Lightness of Being,* pp. 49, 51, 52.
13. Walter Kasper, *Theology and Church* (New York: Crossroad, 1989), p. 51.
14. Hillesum, *An Interrupted Life,* p. 173.
15. Rahner, *The Spirit in the Church,* p. 14.
16. Kundera, *Unbearable Lightness,* p. 41.
17. Ibid., p. 52.
18. Ibid., p. 30.
19. Some Orthodox theologians, e.g., Vladimir Lossky, have criticized the "filioque" theology of the West for reducing the Spirit to the function of a link between the other two Persons and subordinating her to the Son in "contempt of the genuine *perichoresis*" (Congar, *The Word and the Spirit,* p. 113). The personal fullness of the spirit's economic activity is thereby lost.
20. L'Engle, *The Irrational Season,* p. 187.
21. Congar, *The Word and Spirit,* p. 53, also p. 66.
22. Kasper, *Theology and Church,* p. 152.
23. St. Bernard, In *cant. sermo* 8, 2f. (PL 183, 811f.)
24. Congar, *The Word and the Spirit,* p. 116.
25. *Gaudium et Spes* 41,1; 26, 4; and 38,1. Pastoral Constitution on the Church in the

Modern World, *The Documents of Vatican II,* ed. Walter M. Abbott, S.J. (New York: Guild Press, 1966), pp. 199–308.

26. Teilhard de Chardin, *The Divine Milieu,* p. 50.

27. Teilhard de Chardin, *Hymn of the Universe,* p. 123.

28. Teilhard de Chardin, Letter of August 22, 1915.

29. Bill Huebsch, *Spirituality of Wholeness* (Mystic, CT: Twenty-Third Publications, 1989), p. 91.

30. Ibid, p. 101.

31. Ibid., p. 106.

32. Underhill, *The Life of the Spirit and the Life of Today,* p. 64.

33. Ibid., p. 65.

34. "Fiery energies and impulses to the light" is a phrase attributed to Jacob Boehme.

35. Quoted in Underhill, *The Life of the Spirit and the Life of Today,* p. 67.

36. For the concept of sin as "contempt for the vulnerable" I am indebted to Rev. Lynn McLean, associate pastor at Judson Memorial Baptist Church, Minneapolis, Minnesota.

37. Fuchs, *Christian Morality,* p. 100.

38. Congar, *The Word and the Spirit,* p. 55.

CHAPTER 6: BEING AND DOING

Bell, Robert. "Friendships of Men and Women." *Psychology of Women Quarterly* 5/3 (Spring 1981) 402–17.

Bryan, Anne J., and George J. Petrangelo. "Self-Concept and Sex Role Orientation in Adolescence." *Journal of Sex Education and Therapy* 15/1 (Spring 1989) 17–29.

Fortunato, John E. *AIDS, the Spiritual Dilemma.* San Francisco: Harper and Row, 1987.

Grmek, Mirko D. *History of AIDS: Emergence and Origin of a Modern Pandemic.* Translated by Russell C. Maulitz and Jacalyn Duffin. Princeton, NJ: Princeton University Press, 1990.

McGill, Laurilyn, et al. "AIDS: Knowledge, Attitudes, and Risk Characteristics of Teens." *Journal of Sex Education and Therapy* 15/1 (Spring 1989) 30–49.

Tilleraas, Perry. *Circle of Hope: Our Stories of AIDS, Addiction, and Recovery.* Center City, MN: Hazelden, 1990.

1. On ecology of the spirit: Leech, *Spirituality and Pastoral Care,* p. 81.

2. Cited in *Walking on the Water: Women Talk about Spirituality,* ed. Sara Maitland and Jo Garcia (London: Virago, 1983), p. 7.

3. Satir, *The New Peoplemaking,* especially chap. 3.

4. Bell, "Friendships of Men and Women," pp. 402, 405, 408–10, 415–17.

5. McGill et al, "AIDS: Knowledge, Attitudes and Risk Characteristics of Teens," pp. 33–35.

6. Grmek, *History of AIDS,* p. xii.

7. Ibid., p. 197.

8. Ibid., pp. 191–92.

9. Sally Fisher, in Tilleraas, *Circle of Hope,* p. 54.

Index

Abstinence
  biochemical changes, 82
  in older adults, 80–82
Acquired immune deficiency syndrome
  in adolescence, 60, 138
  individual privacy vs. right to know, 140–142
  ministering to people with, 137–144
  moral considerations, 138–139
  Patient Zero, 141–142
Aelred of Rievaulx, on friendship, 137
Agape, 134
Age of grief, 79, 82
Ambiguity
  American aversion to, 97
  in transition periods, 94–97
Anamnesis, 4
Art. *See* Religious art
Asceticism, 20, 29–30
  as change, 119
  to realize Christian freedom, 13
Augustine, St., theory of original sin, 13–14, 123
Authenticity, 21
  asceticism of, 119
Autonomy
  in experiencing the Spirit, 109
  in sexual relationships, 69, 116

Bernard, St., the kiss, 113
Body
  acceptance of, 8, 95
  sacredness of, 88
  taboos, 87
Body image
  adolescents, 52
  women's, 43–45
Breast-feeding, 74–75
Brownmiller, Susan, 43, 44

Campbell, Joseph, on human spiritual growth, 92–93
Celibacy, 29–30, 33
  by priesthood, 34
  vocation vs. lifestyle, 31
Chardin, Teilhard de, 117–118
  The Divine Milieu, 115
Child-free sexual partnerships, 77
Christology, shifting content of, 26–27
Christomonism, 111
Clement of Alexandria, on asceticism, 29
Commitment
  co-defining boundaries, 67–68
  in marriage, 69–73
  nonsexual, 68
  readiness for, 66–67
Communication
  on sexual likes and dislikes, 59
  on sexual orientation, 55, 57–58
  of values, 76
Compassion, spiritual significance of, 139–140
Compulsive behavior, 62–63, 130
Contraception, 64
Council of Trent, definition of sacrament, 23
Creation theology, effect on sexuality mores, 12–13
Cycles of change, 86

Decision-making, sexual, 15, 124–127
Dialectic of the sacred, 24
Discernment in lifestyle choices, 34–36
Divine Milieu, The (de Chardin), 114
Divorce, 34
  remarriage after, 36
Doctrine of God, 104–118
Domination-subordination patterns, 40–41, 47–48, 90
Douglas, Mary, 88

accepting our bodies, 95
  on purity, 91, 92
Dunne, John S., 85
Dunne, John, on human love, 104

Ecstasy, 38, 39–40
Eroticism
  in church art, 29
  older adults, 82
  spiritual growth and, 127–128
Experience of the Spirit, 107–116
  in everyday things, 109–110
  institutional mediation, 112–113
  in moments of crisis, 110
  in sexual experience, 108
  spiritual exercise, 110–111
  theological impediments, 111–112

Familiaris Consortio (John Paul II), 32
Fantasy in sexual expression, 98
Femininity
  cultural standards, 42–43
  family-defined, 45
  hair and clothes considerations, 43–45
Feminist men, 41
Fertility, end of, 80, 81
Fidelity, human vs. God's, 68, 114
Final Payments (Gordon), 90, 91, 131
Food
  disorders, social basis for, 96–97
  liminality and, 96–97
  sexuality and, 12, 96–97
  taboos, 91
  women's body image issues, 44, 97
Friendship
  in Christian theology, 133–134
  functions of, 134–135
  gender and age differences, 136–137
  male-female, 135
Fuchs, Joseph, 122

Gender role, 39
  friendship patterns, 136–137
  reconstructing, 46–47
  social basis for, 40
  taboos, 90
Gender and sex, 9–10
Genital fixation, 70
God
  feminine characteristics, 41
  theological models of, 105–106
Gordon, Mary, *Final Payments*, 90, 91
Gordon, Sol, on sexual identity, 57
Grace, 33–34
  liberating power, 108–109

loving first, 111
  sin and, 119–120

Hillesum, Etty, 84, 98
  on experiencing the Spirit, 107
  hearkening, 109
Holiness as order, 87–88
Homosexuality
  anti-gay-rights position, 58
  church acceptance of, 36
  levels of sexual identity, 40
  spirituality and, 34
  See also Sexual orientation
Hrdy, Sarah, primate studies, 42–43
Huebsch, William, on the created self, 119

Incarnation, 24–25, 27–28
Inner call, 35–36
Intercourse
  first, 59–62
  older adults, 80
  self-transcendence during, 62
  single acts, 122–123
  spiritual meaning, 60
Interiorization, 84
Intimacy, 36–39
  developing, 65–66
  in marriage, 69–70
  spiritual issue, 66

James, William, 17, 35
Jesus
  humanity of, 26, 28, 30
  imitation of, 31
  model for compassion, 140
  sexuality of, 27–30
Jesusology, 111
John Paul II, *Familiaris Consortio*, 32

Kasper, Walter, 109, 113
Kinsey sexuality scale, 56, 57
Kundera, Milan, *The Unbearable Lightness of Being*,
  79, 111

Last Temptation of Christ, The, 27
Leadership and sexual intimacy, 37–38, 84
Leech, Kenneth, ecology of the spirit, 128
L'Engle, Madeleine, 105, 112
Levine, Donald, 97
Lifestyle
  discernment in choices of, 34–36
  vs. vocation, 31
Liminality, 94–99
  disequilibrium with, 95, 98–99
Living together, 67

Love
  after a loss, 77
  caritas vs. eros, 48
  definition, 85
  learning self-, 132
  in male-female relationships, 47–48
  vocation to, 26, 32

Mackin, Theodore, 105
Malakoi, 122
Maney, Sarah, self-worth prayer, 133
Marriage
  commitment in, 69–73
  effect of parenthood on, 75
  friendship in, 136
  institutionalization of, 121–122
  involvement/detachment cycle, 70–71
  sacramentality of, 71–72
  second, 36
  as vocation, 31
  women's expectations of, 71
Masculinity, 40–42
  marginalization of men from family, 42
  mid-life crisis, 82
  phallus vs. penis, 70
Masturbation. *See* Self-pleasuring
Medicalization of women's bodies, 46–47
Menarche, 53–54
Menopause, physical changes during, 81
Mentors
  during spiritual growth, 20–21
  for older adults, 83–84
Ministry
  qualities of effective, 142–144
  to people with AIDS, 137–144
Moral agency, 41
  adolescents, 53
Morality
  forced conformity to, 121
  New Testament view, 122
  questioning one's own, 120–121
  shift from conventional to internal, 63–64
  taboos and, 90
  theology of, 118–126
Moral order, dealing with threats to, 89
Mystery of God, 23
  in sacramental view of reality, 24
Mysticism
  ambiguity and, 97
  experiences of union, 21–22

Nelson, James, on male sexuality, 70

Older adults
  friendships, 136
  sexual concerns, 79–85

Once-born personality, 35
Oral sex, 59

Pagels, Elaine, 12
Parenting, 74–77
  spiritual significance, 73–74
Paschal mystery, life passages as, 116–118
Pastoral Constitution on the Church in the Modern
  World, 124
Paul, St., on celibacy, 29
Penelope's robe metaphor, 3–4
Pollution beliefs, 89, 90
Power
  gender differences, 46
  sexual, 22, 52–53
  of taboos, 92–93
  use of personal, 101
Pregnancy
  sexuality of childbirth, 74
  spiritual significance, 73–74
Puberty, 51–52
  adapting to body changes, 52
  parent-to-peer emotional transition, 54–55
  See also Sexual partnerships
Purification, 20–21
  rituals of, 88
Purity, 91–92

Rahner, Karl, 108
  experiencing the Spirit, 109–110
  sacramental event, 25
  on sacramental marriage, 72
Reconciliation in gender relations, 47
Relationships
  lost or failed, 77–79
  quest for God in, 105
  See also Sexual partnerships
Religious art, eroticism in, 29
Renaming, 99–102, 129–130, 143, 145
Repressed behavior, 37, 120
Responsible sex, 63–64
Rilke, Rainer Maria, 86
  on incarnation, 25
Rites of Passage (Van Gennep), 95
Ritual
  of purification, 88
  of segregation, 95
Roman Catholic Church, political vs. sexual
  agenda, 123

Sacramentality
  changing definitions, 23
  of human experience, 22–23
  of marriage, 71–72

of reality, 24
of sex, 25, 85
Sarrel, Lorna, and Sarrel, Phillip, sexual unfolding, 52
Schillebeeckx, Edward
  on developing a Christology, 26
  Jesusology, 111
Scrupulosity, 93
Self-actualization, diversity of forms, 58
Self-awareness in establishing intimacy, 37
Self-esteem, 130–133
  articulating negative feelings, 131–132
  developing positive, 59
  in people with AIDS, 143
  victimization and, 131
Self-pleasuring
  during childhood, 75
  during puberty, 54
  older adults, 80
Semenarche, 53–54
Sex
  biochemical changes during, 39
  changing ideology of, 2
  communicating likes and dislikes, 59–60
  and death, 4, 139
  definition, 9
  experiencing the Spirit in, 108
  gender and, 9–10
  goodness of, 11–12
  male attitude toward, 65
  for older adults, 79–85
  overcoming negative attitudes, 54
  place and value of, 63
  reductionism, 1–2
  religious valorization of, 11–14
Sex education, 75–76, 128
Sexual dysfunction, 62
Sexual identity, 39–40
  See also Gender role
Sexuality
  cultural constraints, 10
  definition, 9
  discriminating between good and evil, 33
  history of attitude toward, 10–11, 121–122
  immanence-transcendence experiences, 104
  life experience, 4–5
  loss of, 1–2
  reductionism, 7–8
  women's acceptance of, 59
Sexual orientation, 57–59
  communication during puberty, 55
Sexual partnership, effect of friendship on, 135
Sexual partnerships
  love in, 47–48
  retaining autonomy, 69, 116
  sacramental function, 116, 118

Sexual unfolding, 50
  coping with sexual dysfunction, 62
  developmental tasks, 52–66
  individual experiences, 51
Shirley Valentine (movie), 1, 98
Sin
  models of, 119–120
  original, 13–14, 30, 123
  sexual potential for, 13–14, 118–119
Spidlik, Thomas, stages of spiritual growth, 19–22
Spirit
  as cosmic creator, 114–115
  function of, 27
  linking sexuality with, 114
  theology of, ecclesial effect, 113–114
  See also Experience of the Spirit
Spiritual growth
  disciplines for, 129–130
  eroticism and, 127–128
  shedding taboos, 92–93
  stages of, 19–22
Spirituality
  as progress toward maturity, 49–50
  response and source of, 19
  sacramental, 18
  theological language, 10
  types of, 16–18
Spiritually active persons, formation of, 127–130
Spiritual-sexual integration
  causal connection, 15
  hermeneutical principle, 8–9
  religious growth through, 145
  to combat sexual abuse, 128–129
  See also Theology of sexuality
Stayton, William, erotic response model, 56, 57–58
Steinberg, Leo, 28
Stevens, Wallace, "The World as Meditation," 4
Szasz, Thomas, 97

Taboos
  food, 91
  morals and, 90
  power of, 92–93
  sexual, 32, 119–120, 121
  shedding, 92–94, 121
Temptation, 30
Theology of sexuality, 2–3, 30, 123–124
Tillich, Paul, 77
Trinity, 105
Turner, Brian, on food disorders, 96–97
Twice-born personality, 17, 35, 110

Unbearable Lightness of Being, The (Kundera), 79, 86, 111
Underhill, Evelyn, sin as conservatism, 119, 120

Van Gennep, Arnold, *Rites of Passage*, 95
Vatican II, concept of sacrament, 23
Violence against women, 42
Virginity
  loss of, religious significance, 60–61
  medieval period, 91
Vocation
  of friendship, 134
  sexual, 32
  spiritual, 32
  theology of, 35–36

to love, 26, 32
vs. lifestyle, 31
See also Inner call
Vulnerability
  after failed relationship, 77
  expressing with friends, 134
  intimacy and, 65–66

Wainwright, Geoffrey, types of spirituality, 16–18
Women's movement
  accepting sexuality, 59
  contribution to spiritual growth, 20
  empowerment, 22
"World as Meditation, The" (Stevens), 4